YEAR-ROUND
SLOW
100 Favorite Recipes for Every Season
COOKER

INA CHENEY

To Koby

Text © 2013 by Dina Cheney

Photographs © 2013 by Andrew Hugh Purcell except for the following pages: 7, 31, 38, 146, 178, 199, 211 by Scott Phillips, © 2013 by The Taunton Press, Inc.

The Taunton Press
Inspiration for hands-on living®

The Taunton Press, Inc., 63 South Main Street, PO Box 5506, Newtown, CT 06470-5506
e-mail: tp@taunton.com

Editor: Carolyn Mandarano
Copy editor: Nina Rynd Whitnah
Indexer: Barbara Mortenson
Cover and interior design: Kimberly Adis
Layout: Kimberly Adis
Photographers: Andrew Hugh Purcell and Scott Phillips
Food stylist: Carrie Purcell
Prop stylist: Paige Hicks

The following names/manufacturers appearing in *Year-Round Slow Cooker* are trademarks: Ball®, Bob's Red Mill®, Cointreau®, Corona®, Geeta's®, Guinness®, Looza®, Lyle's Golden Syrup®, Microplane®, Minute®, Pillivuyt®, PureNotes™, Silk®, Tabasco®

Library of Congress Cataloging-in-Publication Data in progress
ISBN: 978-1-60085-490-3

Printed in the United States of America
10 9 8 7 6 5 4 3 2 1

Acknowledgments

WHAT A FUN, CREATIVE CHALLENGE it's been to modernize and freshen up slow-cooker fare with colorful, flavorful, seasonal produce! Thanks to my super-intelligent, kind, and lovely-to-work-with editor, Carolyn Mandarano at The Taunton Press—the ultimate collaborator! Thanks also to my dear friend, Rebecca Freedman, who introduced me to Carolyn and has always championed my work.

Cassie Bowman (who is a font of book ideas!), as well as my over-the-top brilliant and loving mom, Harriet Cheney, tested out several of the recipes—thank you, thank you.

Thanks to photographer Andrew Hugh Purcell; food stylist Carrie Purcell; prop stylist Paige Hicks; book designer Kim Adis; and Alison Wilkes and Katy Binder at Taunton.

Hamilton Beach provided me with a wealth of reliable, easy-to-use, and lightweight slow cookers—indispensable for developing these dishes! Thanks to Melissa's World Variety Produce for supplying me with sorrel and fava beans out of season.

A bunch of friends and family members have constantly supplied love and support. In particular, I'd love to thank my sister, Jackie; father, David; grandmother, Thelma; my terrific in-laws; my husband's grandmother, Yolanda; dear friend Abby; and children, Max and Abe. Perhaps my heartiest thanks of all goes to my husband and closest friend, Koby. He's always wholeheartedly encouraged my career, even when that meant devoting many of his weekend and vacation days to watching our preschoolers so I could work. Now, that's love!

Contents

Fresh Ingredients Meet the Slow Cooker

SLOW COOKERS CAN TURN HUMBLE INGREDIENTS INTO UNCTUOUS, mouth-watering dishes worthy of a five-star restaurant—really. Since they cook unattended, you can leave the house while a rich, layered dish simmers to perfection. After the dish has cooked, it can be kept "warm," allowing different family members to eat at different times. And, since 6-quart and larger models can prepare enough food for six or more people, you'll likely end up with leftovers.

Some home cooks use these hard-working appliances only for fall and winter meals, and others associate them with fare that's mushy, bland, watery, or brown. Many slow-cooker recipes call for processed ingredients, including bouillon cubes, bottled sauce, and spice packets. Fresh seasonal produce is nowhere to be found.

I set out to change that thinking by writing *Year-Round Slow Cooker.* In the following pages, you'll find recipes for modern, flavorful, colorful entrées and desserts featuring fresh produce, all organized by season. What you *won't* see are soup mix and store-bought sauces. Throughout the book, I've also included recipes for accompaniments (which are not made in

the slow cooker) to serve alongside your slow-cooked masterpieces.

I've incorporated fresh, seasonal ingredients in myriad ways. I'll often cook hardier vegetables fully in the slow cooker, placing them in the bottom of the insert. With delicate vegetables, I'll either cook them quickly on the stove or add them to the slow cooker near the end of the overall cooking process. In some cases, I'll lend a fresh note to a dish after it finishes cooking by topping or serving it with a garnish of herbs or a salsa, chutney, or sauce prepared with seasonal produce.

To inspire your cooking throughout the year, each chapter begins with a list of seasonal fruits and vegetables featured in the recipes in that chapter. I've also included detailed information on fruits and vegetables in sidebars called "Spotlight On...."

To ensure that you make the most delicious dishes possible, I've sprinkled sidebars called "Slow Cooker Secret" throughout the book, as well. Here, you'll find tips for turning out scrumptious slow-cooked food. After reading these tips, you, too, will be a slow-cooker pro.

Once you start preparing these recipes, I predict that you'll move your slow cooker from the dusty basement to a prime spot on the kitchen counter—and use it year-round.

THE SLOW COOKER LIFESTYLE

When I began working on this book, I aimed to create "set it and forget it" recipes that would cook for the equivalent of a full workday. I quickly realized that such a goal was not attainable if I wanted to create dishes that were delicious and showcased seasonal ingredients.

Some ingredients, such as beef brisket, pork shoulder, and dried beans, are ideal when cooked for 8 hours or more. Most do best when cooked for shorter periods of time, though. Fish cooks very quickly, in about 1 hour. Desserts take anywhere from 2 to 4 hours (more than that and they'll usually overcook or burn due to their high sugar content). Chicken cooks perfectly in about 4 hours; more than 6 hours and it becomes tough.

That's why I recommend making long-cooking dishes on workdays and fish, chicken, and dessert on weekends—or even after your workday ends. For certain dishes, such as brisket and poached pears, try to make them a day (or more) ahead of time; as the meat and fruit sit in the sauce, they soak up flavors.

CHOOSING AND USING A SLOW COOKER

Slow cookers consist of an insert (crock); a base, which contains a heating element; and a cord and plug, for plugging into an electrical outlet. The inserts are thick and heavy, with the heating elements well insulated in the base units. Because the heat levels are low, food in the crock can withstand lengthy cooking times.

There are many types of slow cookers on the market, from small (3-quart crocks) to large (crocks up to 7 quarts). Inserts can be round, rectangular, or oval shaped. I find the most versatile to be a 6-quart model with an oval-shaped crock, and that's what I used to test all of the slow cooker recipes in this book.

Some models feature a stovetop-safe insert, which you can use for browning and cooking—no need to dirty a sauté pan. These slow cookers also happen to be a cinch to clean. I highly recommend them. However, since most slow cookers do not feature a stovetop-safe insert, I developed all of the recipes in this book with a traditional model and browned ingredients in a sauté pan or saucepan.

If your slow cooker contains a stovetop-safe insert, be sure to remove any burnt bits of food after sautéing (if not, they'll transmit a burnt flavor to your dish). Also be aware that dishes will likely cook more quickly than my recipes indicate, since the insert will be hot when you begin the slow-cooking process.

Before plugging in your slow cooker, read the manual to learn how to use it safely and how to care for it. Make sure to note whether the insert is dishwasher safe and whether it needs to cool to room temperature before being cleaned.

Since slow cookers cook at a low heat (around 195° to 205°F), there's a chance that food could end up in the food safety "danger zone" (between 40° and 140°F for more than 2 hours). To prevent this, don't add frozen ingredients directly to the slow cooker (thaw and drain them first), and don't remove the lid more than absolutely necessary (each time you do, the temperature will drop by about 20° to 25°F).

Don't fill your slow cooker to its capacity. Instead, fill all models about two-thirds full. Try not to cook especially large pieces of meat in the slow cooker, and use an instant-read thermometer and the USDA meat temperature guidelines to ensure meat is cooked through (see the sidebar on the facing page). Don't keep food on the "warm" setting for more than 2 hours (even if fully cooked), and never reheat food in the slow cooker.

Finally, treat your appliance as you would any electrical device: Avoid getting it wet before or during use, and keep it out of the reach of children.

ROAD MAP FOR MAKING FLAVORFUL SLOW-COOKED FOOD

Although slow cookers are a convenient means of making one-pot meals, you will still need to do a bit of advance prep work to turn out the most flavorful food. Usually this amounts to building a sauce on the stove and, sometimes, browning meat (see "Browning Meat" on p. 178). Here is a basic road map to the techniques for most of the savory dishes in this book. After doing this a few times, the process will become second nature.

■ **Dredge meat in seasoned flour and brown on the stovetop.** Combine flour with spices in a bowl, then dredge meat in this mixture, shaking off and reserving the excess flour. Heat the amount of oil called for in the recipe in a 10-inch sauté pan over medium-high heat. When hot, add the meat and cook until golden brown on both sides, being careful not to crowd the pan (you may need to brown in batches). Transfer the meat to the slow cooker.

■ **Sauté vegetables and add the reserved flour.** Add the aromatics (onions, garlic, etc.) to the hot pan and sauté, stirring with a wooden spoon, until softened, about 5 minutes. (Using a wooden spoon helps to dislodge flavorful bits left from browning the meat and doesn't scratch the pan.) If you don't have the exact amount of vegetables called for in my recipes, don't worry; you can always just sauté what you have on hand. Next, whisk in tomato paste and any remaining flour-and-spice mixture, simmering and stirring until the white flour disappears; this typically takes about a minute.

You're adding a lot of flour here to ensure that your sauce—after slow cooking—will be thick enough. Since slow cookers cook at a low temperature and crocks are covered during the cooking process, very little liquid evaporates. Plus, ingredients release a lot of liquid during slow cooking. The solution is to over-thicken your sauce before you begin slow-cooking your dish. This way, you'll end up with a sauce that's the perfect consistency—and not watery.

■ **Finish making the sauce.** If wine or beer is called for in a recipe, I recommend moving the pan off the heat before adding it (for safety). Once the liquid is added, return the pan to the heat, raise the heat to high, and simmer, whisking, until the alcohol reduces a bit and the sauce looks relatively smooth and thick, about 3 minutes. Add

MINIMUM INTERNAL TEMPERATURES FOR DONENESS

The USDA recommends the following minimum internal temperatures for meat and poultry; wait until they reach at least these temperatures before removing them from the heat. To gauge temperature, stick an instant-read thermometer in the center of a piece of meat—not touching bone.

■ Raw beef, pork, lamb, and veal steaks, chops, and roasts: 145°F.
■ Raw ground beef, pork, lamb, and veal: 160°F.
■ All poultry: 165°F.

any other liquids called for in the recipe, such as stock and juice, and continue cooking over high heat until the sauce is thickened, about another 4 minutes (see the photos on the facing page). Pour this sauce over the meat in the slow cooker, cover, and cook as directed.

POWER INGREDIENTS

As you read through these recipes, you'll notice that I rely on certain ingredients over and over again. Here is a list of the power players you will likely want to stock in your pantry.

Staples

- Unbleached all-purpose flour
- Low-sodium chicken and vegetable stock
- Vegetable oil, olive oil, and cooking spray
- Unsalted butter
- Honey and granulated sugar (for balancing flavors)
- Pectin (for preserves)
- White arborio rice
- Steel-cut groats
- Tapioca starch (for thickening desserts)
- Instant white rice (for savory rice dishes)
- Dried beans and lentils

Flavor boosters

- Tomato paste and canned tomatoes (without basil or other flavorings)
- Mustard (Dijon and yellow)
- Mango chutney
- Pomegranate molasses
- Dried wild mushrooms
- Canned chipotle chiles en adobo sauce
- Spices
- Dried herbs (especially hardy, woody ones, such as oregano, thyme, and sage)
- Vanilla bean paste or extract
- Alcohol (beer, wine, sherry)

- Fruit juice or nectar
- Garlic and onions
- Fresh ginger
- Curry paste
- Olives
- Sauerkraut
- Bacon
- Sausage

POWER TOOLS

Beyond a slow cooker, you'll need very few tools to prepare the recipes in this book, but I've found the following items to be very helpful.

General

- Heavy-duty aluminum foil
- Large spoon or ladle for skimming off grease
- Whisk
- Wooden spoons
- 10-inch, heavy sauté pan
- Kitchen twine
- Kitchen shears
- Cheesecloth
- Tongs
- Colander
- Large slotted spoon or spider
- Microplane® zester
- Vegetable peeler

For handling meat

- Turkey lifters
- Sharp boning knife (for cutting off fat and skin)

For desserts and puddings

- Baking dish that fits inside your slow cooker (I love the white Pillivuyt® 10½- x 7½- x 2-inch, 1½-quart, medium-size, deep oval model)
- Trivet or rack that fits inside your slow cooker
- Kettle for quickly boiling water
- Thick rubber bands (for securing foil over a baking dish when making puddings)

MAKING A SAUCE

Building your sauce on the stovetop before slow cooking couldn't be simpler—and guarantees a flavorful dish that's not at all watery.

Slice, dice, or chop onions and other aromatics as indicated in the recipe.

Sauté the aromatics until soft, usually between 4 and 7 minutes.

Whisk the thick, gummy tomato paste and reserved flour mixture just until the white flour disappears.

After adding the wine or beer, simmer the sauce—whisking constantly—until it becomes smooth, thick, and uniform.

After 3 or 4 minutes, the sauce will thicken to the correct consistency before it's ready for the slow cooker.

WINTER

SEASONAL SPOTLIGHT

- Avocados
- Coconuts
- Collard greens
- Ginger
- Jerusalem artichokes

- Kiwis
- Lemons
- Limes
- Mangos
- Oranges
- Plantains

- Pomegranates
- Tangerines
- Winter squash

Apricot chicken with carrots

SERVES 4

Zest of 1 lemon (yellow part only)

1 pound carrots, peeled and cut into ⅓- by 2-inch pieces

30 whole dried apricots (preferably with sulfur, for a pretty color)

¼ cup plus 1 tablespoon all-purpose flour

¼ teaspoon ground cinnamon

¼ teaspoon ground coriander

⅛ teaspoon ground ginger

⅛ teaspoon ground cardamom

⅛ teaspoon ground cayenne pepper

1 teaspoon coarse salt

20 grinds black pepper

2½ pounds bone-in, skinless chicken thighs (about 8 thighs)

2 tablespoons vegetable oil

1 tablespoon unsalted butter

2¼ cups finely chopped white onions (about 2 small)

1½ tablespoons minced garlic

2 tablespoons tomato paste

1 cup apricot nectar, such as Looza®

¼ cup fresh-squeezed, strained lemon juice

½ cup low-sodium chicken stock

¼ cup toasted pine nuts, for garnish (optional)

¼ cup finely chopped fresh cilantro, parsley, or mint leaves, for garnish (optional)

Perfect for Rosh Hashanah, this stew is delicious served over couscous or brown rice pilaf with fresh cilantro or parsley. Feel free to use oil for the butter.

1. Place the lemon peel on a piece of cheesecloth, form into a "purse," and secure with kitchen twine. Add it to the slow cooker, along with the carrots and apricots. Place the flour and all of the spices in a large bowl and mix well. Add the chicken and coat well, shaking off the excess and reserving any remaining flour.

2. Heat 1 tablespoon of oil and the butter in a 10-inch sauté pan over medium-high heat. When the butter is melted, brown the chicken in two batches, about 11 minutes total; add the remaining 1 tablespoon oil if the pan becomes dry. Transfer the chicken to the slow cooker.

3. Add the onions and garlic to the hot pan, and cook until the onions are softened, scraping the bottom of the pan with a wooden spoon, about 3 minutes. Stir in the tomato paste and reserved flour and whisk well until the flour disappears, about a minute. Add the nectar, lemon juice, and stock; bring to a boil. Boil for 2 minutes, then pour the sauce over the chicken in the slow cooker. Submerge the chicken.

4. Cover and cook on low until the chicken is cooked through and the carrots are tender, 5 to 6 hours. Serve, garnishing each portion with nuts and herbs, if desired.

Brisket with pomegranate, red wine, and caramelized onions

SERVES 6

¼ cup plus 2 tablespoons pomegranate molasses

2 tablespoons Dijon mustard

2 tablespoons minced garlic

1 teaspoon ground coriander

1 teaspoon coarse salt

8 grinds black pepper

One 3-pound beef brisket

3 tablespoons vegetable oil

2 red onions, halved and cut into ½-inch-thick rings

3 tablespoons tomato paste

3 tablespoons all-purpose flour

½ cup red wine, such as Zinfandel

One 14-ounce can whole peeled tomatoes, with juices

½ cup low-sodium chicken stock

¼ cup fresh-squeezed, strained orange juice

2 tablespoons honey

¾ cup pomegranate seeds, at room temperature, for garnish

Pomegranate molasses and seeds add seasonal flair and a fresh, sweet-tart taste to this brisket, ideal for the Jewish holidays and other special occasions. Prepare this dish a day or two in advance to allow the flavors to meld and the meat to become more tender and flavorful.

Pomegranate molasses is available at many gourmet grocers and at Mideastern markets.

1. Put ¼ cup of the pomegranate molasses, the mustard, garlic, coriander, salt, and pepper in the slow cooker and use a wooden spoon to mix well. Add the meat and turn to coat with the mixture (use your fingers to smear the mixture all over the meat).

2. Heat 2 tablespoons of the oil in a 10-inch, heavy sauté pan over medium heat. When hot, add the onions and cook, stirring occasionally, until golden brown, limp, and sweet, about 20 minutes (discard any strips of red onion skin that separate from the flesh). Pour the onions on top of the meat.

3. Add the remaining tablespoon of oil, plus the tomato paste and flour to the pan. Stir until no white flour is visible, about 1 minute. Remove the pan from the heat and carefully add the wine; return the pan to the heat, raise the heat to high, and simmer for about 2 minutes, whisking into a smooth, thick sauce. Add the

continued

remaining 2 tablespoons pomegranate molasses, the tomatoes with juices, stock, orange juice, and honey, and use a potato masher to gently mash the tomatoes. Boil until smooth and relatively thick, about 4 minutes, then pour over the meat-onion mixture.

4. Cover and cook on low until tender, about 8 hours. Carefully transfer the meat to a cutting board, and let rest for about 10 minutes. With a large shallow spoon or ladle, skim the fat off the top of the cooking juices. Cut the meat against the grain into roughly ⅓-inch-thick slices, mix it back into the sauce, and serve, garnished with the pomegranate seeds.

SPOTLIGHT ON

POMEGRANATES

Pomegranates are large, hard, pink or red round fruits. You only eat their arils, pulp-encased seeds that resemble rubies and boast a sweet-tart berry flavor.

To remove the arils, halve the pomegranate horizontally, place it in a large water-filled bowl, and pull the arils out from the bitter white membranes. You can also thwack the backside of each half with your fist to knock out some arils; these will keep in the fridge for up to 5 days. Or purchase already-removed arils, which I find to be worth the extra price. Follow the use-by date on the package for freshness.

If you buy whole pomegranates, look for heavy, firm, brightly colored fruits. Store them in the fridge for up to 2 months or in a cool, dark place for up to 1 month.

Japanese-style chicken soup with udon noodles and lime

SERVES 4

1-quart low-sodium chicken stock

2 bags of unflavored green tea, such as Sencha

¼ cup fresh-squeezed, strained lime juice

One 3½-pound whole chicken, butterflied and pressed flat (skin and bone left on)

1 large carrot, peeled and cut into tenths

1 large parsnip, peeled and cut into eighths

6 trimmed scallions, 3 cut into thirds and 3 thinly sliced

1 stalk celery, cut into sixths

2-inch piece fresh ginger, peeled and cut into sixths

1 teaspoon coarse salt

About 6 ounces uncooked udon or soba noodles (or spaghetti)

This healthy, one-pot meal is a Japanese-inspired twist on chicken soup. Add more low-sodium chicken stock for additional volume, and stir in a bit of wasabi paste for heat. To butterfly the chicken, use sharp kitchen shears to cut through the breastbone. Also, if your parsnip is very large, remove the hard core, which will be tough.

1. Heat the stock in a microwave-safe bowl in the microwave until very hot, 1 to 2 minutes. Add the tea bags and steep for 5 minutes; remove and discard the tea bags. Pour the broth plus the lime juice into the slow cooker. Add the chicken, carrots, parsnips, large pieces of scallions, celery, ginger, and salt. Press down on the chicken to submerge in the liquid. Cover and cook on low until the chicken is cooked through, about 4 hours.

2. Carefully transfer the chicken to a cutting board. Set a large hand-held strainer over a heavy medium-size saucepan and pour the broth and vegetables into it. Transfer the solids to another cutting board. Bring the broth to a boil over high heat.

3. While the broth comes to a boil, discard the ginger, celery, and scallions. Finely chop the carrots and parsnips, and set aside. Remove and discard the chicken skin and bones. Shred the meat and set aside.

4. Once the broth comes to a boil, add the carrots, parsnip, and noodles; stir and simmer until the pasta is cooked through and the root vegetables are tender, 5 to 8 minutes. Stir in the shredded chicken and thinly sliced scallions, and serve.

BBQ mango baby back ribs

SERVES 4

3½ pounds pork baby back ribs, cut into two pieces to fit into the slow cooker

One 10-ounce jar high-quality mango chutney (about 1 cup), such as Major Grey's

½ cup thick mango nectar, such as Looza

One 14-ounce can whole peeled tomatoes, with juice

¼ cup fresh-squeezed, strained lime juice

2 tablespoons light brown sugar

2 tablespoons Dijon mustard

1 tablespoon cider vinegar

1 tablespoon low-sodium tamari soy sauce

1 tablespoon adobo sauce from a can of chipotle chiles en adobo

1 teaspoon coarse salt

½ teaspoon chili powder

¼ teaspoon Tabasco® green pepper sauce

1 mango, diced, for serving

Diced fresh mango, mango chutney, and mango nectar work together to give this meaty, saucy dish an amped-up fruit flavor. If you like, feel free to tailor the heat level to your taste. To simplify the recipe, use a purchased mango barbecue sauce and skip reducing the sauce after the ribs have cooked. To lacquer the ribs, broil them after you remove them from the slow cooker.

1. Lay the ribs—bone side visible—against the sides of the slow cooker insert, lining it.

2. Add the remaining ingredients (except the mango) to a medium-size saucepan, stir well, and heat over high. Bring to a boil, and boil for about 15 minutes, gently mashing the tomatoes with a potato masher, until the sauce is reduced to about 2½ cups. Pour over the ribs to cover. Cover and cook on low until tender, 6 to 8 hours.

3. Carefully transfer the ribs to a large serving platter and cover with foil. Let the sauce sit in the slow cooker for about 5 minutes, then use a large spoon or ladle to skim the fat off the surface. Pour the sauce into a medium-size saucepan, and bring it to a boil over high heat. Cook until reduced to about 1½ cups, about 15 minutes. Pour the thickened sauce over the ribs, sprinkle the diced mango on top, and serve.

Latin American seafood stew with lime and coconut

SERVES 4 TO 6

2 tablespoons vegetable oil

2¼ cups finely chopped red onions (about 1)

2 cups finely chopped red bell peppers (about 1)

2 tablespoons plus 2 teaspoons peeled, minced fresh ginger

2 tablespoons plus 2 teaspoons minced garlic

1½ teaspoons minced jalapeño (seeds and membranes removed)

¼ cup all-purpose flour

3 tablespoons tomato paste

1 tablespoon liquid from a can of chipotle chiles en adobo

½ cup plus 2 tablespoons mild beer, such as Corona®

One 28-ounce can whole peeled tomatoes

One 13½-ounce can light coconut milk

½ cup fresh-squeezed, strained lime juice

1½ teaspoons coarse salt, divided

15 grinds black pepper, divided

1½ pounds fresh cod fillets, bones removed, cut into 6 portions

1 pound extra-large shrimp, deveined and peeled (tails left on)

Chopped fresh cilantro leaves, for serving

Garlic toasts, for garnish (optional)

Lime and coconut add tropical flair to this seafood stew, which you can garnish with garlic toasts. Seafood can overcook easily, so check for doneness starting about 1½ hours through cooking.

1. Heat the oil in a 10-inch, heavy sauté pan over medium-high heat. When hot, add the onions, bell peppers, 2 tablespoons of the ginger, 2 tablespoons of the garlic, and ½ teaspoon of the jalapeño. Sauté, stirring with a wooden spoon, until the onions are softened, about 5 minutes. Whisk in the flour, tomato paste, and chipotle liquid, and simmer until the flour disappears, no more than 1 minute.

2. Move the pan off the heat, then add ½ cup of the beer. Return the pan to the heat and raise the heat to high. Simmer for 2 minutes, then add the tomatoes, coconut milk, ¼ cup of the lime juice, 1 teaspoon of the salt, and 5 grinds of the pepper. Simmer for another 2 minutes, breaking up the tomatoes a bit with the back of the spoon, and pour into the slow cooker. Set aside.

3. In a baking dish, combine the remaining 2 teaspoons ginger, remaining 2 teaspoons garlic, remaining teaspoon jalapeño, remaining 2 tablespoons beer, and remaining ¼ cup lime juice. Add the cod and shrimp, and mix well but gently to minimize breaking up the cod. Season with the remaining ½ teaspoon of salt and the remaining 10 grinds of pepper, and pour the fish and all of the marinade into the slow cooker. Stir well, submerging the fish.

4. Cover the slow cooker and cook on high until the seafood is cooked through (but not tough or overcooked), 1½ to 2 hours. Serve the stew in shallow bowls and sprinkle with fresh cilantro. Serve with garlic toasts, if desired.

SLOW COOKER SECRET

CONVERTING SLOW-COOKER RECIPES FOR THE OVEN OR STOVE

Although slow cooker recipes won't turn out exactly the same if they're cooked in the oven or on the stovetop, you can use one of those cooking methods by following some general guidelines.

- Add more liquid. Since liquid evaporates when exposed to dry, higher heat, you'll need more in order to cook food and still have sauce left over.

- Plan on the dish taking roughly half the time on the stove or in the oven than it will take in the slow cooker.

- Keep more fat and skin on meat to help retain moisture (though I still like to remove chicken skin when braising).

- On the stove, bring food to a boil over high heat, then cover the pot and immediately reduce the heat to low or medium low. For the oven, cook food (covered) at about 300° to 350°F.

Brazilian black bean and sausage stew with oranges and collard greens

SERVES 4 TO 6

½ pound sliced bacon, finely chopped

3 spicy fresh pork sausages (scant ¾ pound), casings removed

3 sweet fresh pork sausages (scant ¾ pound) casings removed

Two 15½-ounce cans black beans, rinsed and drained

1 red onion, coarsely chopped

2 red bell peppers, coarsely chopped

5 whole cloves garlic

¼ cup tomato paste

3 tablespoons all-purpose flour

½ cup mild beer, such as Corona

½ cup fresh-squeezed, strained orange juice

1 cup low-sodium chicken stock

3 dried bay leaves

5 cups collard greens, stems removed and leaves finely chopped (about 1 large bunch)

2½ cups cooked long-grain rice, for serving

2 navel oranges, cut into wedges, for serving

Here's a very quick, easy twist on *feijoada*, the Brazilian national dish, served over rice with orange wedges. Unlike traditional feijoada, all of the ingredients in this recipe are readily available at grocery stores.

Kitchen shears make quick work of chopping the bacon and removing the sausage casings. To save time, chop the vegetables while the meat browns.

1. Place the bacon in a cold, 10-inch, heavy sauté pan and heat over medium heat. Cook until most of the fat renders, about 6 minutes. Raise the heat to medium high and continue to cook until the bacon is barely crisp, about another 3 minutes. Add the sausage, breaking it up with a wooden spoon, and cook until it no longer looks raw, about another 9 minutes. Transfer all of the meat to the slow cooker (keeping the fat in the pan). Add the beans to the slow cooker and mix well.

2. Add the onions, peppers, and garlic to the pan with the hot fat, and sauté until the onions are softened, about 5 minutes. Whisk in the tomato paste and flour and cook until the flour disappears, no more than 1 minute. Remove the pan from the heat, add the beer and orange juice, and return the pan to the heat. Raise the heat to high. Simmer for 3 minutes, then add the stock and bay leaves. Simmer for 2 minutes more, then pour over the bean-meat mixture in the slow cooker.

3. Cover and cook on low until the stew is aromatic, about 5 hours. Remove and discard the bay leaves. Stir in the collard greens, cover, and raise the heat to high. Cook until the greens are tender, 30 to 40 minutes. Serve over rice with orange wedges on the side.

COLLARD GREENS

A member of the cabbage family, collards are hardy bitter greens that are delicious when braised with plenty of liquid. To prep them for cooking, cut out and discard the tough stems, and thinly slice the leaves. Look for vibrantly colored, crisp leaves with no yellow spots; store them in the fridge for 3 to 5 days.

Lentils with garam masala, coconut, and pomegranate seeds

SERVES 10
(MAKES ABOUT 10 CUPS)

1 pound dried green lentils, rinsed and picked over (about 2 cups)

2 tablespoons vegetable oil

2¼ cups finely chopped red onions (about 1 large)

¼ cup carrots, finely chopped (about 1)

2 tablespoons minced garlic

2 tablespoons minced fresh ginger

Scant 2 teaspoons minced jalapeño (seeds and membranes removed)

1½ teaspoons garam masala

½ teaspoon turmeric

¼ cup plus 1 tablespoon mango chutney, such as Geeta's®

¼ cup tomato paste

2 tablespoons all-purpose flour

6 cups low-sodium vegetable or chicken stock

3 tablespoons fresh-squeezed, strained lime juice

One 13½-ounce can coconut milk (not low fat), shaken before opening

½ teaspoon coarse salt

¼ cup shredded unsweetened coconut

1 cup pomegranate seeds, for garnish

½ cup plus 2 tablespoons finely chopped, fresh cilantro leaves, for garnish

10 lime wedges, for serving

Cucumber Raita, for serving (recipe on p. 131; optional)

Naan, for serving (optional)

Like a soup or stew, Indian dal features a delicious broth, as does this flavorful, creamy vegetarian take. Studded with jewel-like pomegranate seeds, this dish should be paired with raita (cucumber yogurt sauce) and naan bread for the most authentic dinner. Be sure to add the salt later in the cooking process so the lentils have a chance to soften.

1. Add the lentils to the slow cooker.

2. Heat the oil in a medium-size heavy saucepan over medium-high heat. When hot, add the onions, carrots, garlic, ginger, jalapeño, garam masala, and turmeric and sauté until the onions are softened, about 5 minutes. Whisk in the chutney, tomato paste, and flour and cook until the flour is no longer visible, about 1 minute.

3. Add the stock and lime juice, raise the heat to high, and bring to a boil, whisking. Remove the pot from the heat and stir in the coconut milk. Pour over the lentils. Cover and cook on low until the lentils are tender, 6 to 8 hours. Stir in the salt and coconut. Garnish each portion with pomegranate seeds, cilantro, and a lime wedge, and serve.

Chicken tagine with preserved lemons and Jerusalem artichokes

SERVES 4

1 pound Jerusalem artichokes (sunchokes), peeled and cut into roughly 1-inch pieces (about 2½ cups)

½ teaspoon cumin, divided

½ teaspoon ground coriander, divided

½ teaspoon ground cinnamon, divided

¼ teaspoon cayenne, divided

½ teaspoon coarse salt

4 grinds black pepper

⅓ cup all-purpose flour

3 pounds bone-in, skinless chicken thighs (about 8), excess fat trimmed

2 tablespoons olive oil

1½ cups finely chopped yellow or white onions

6 large cloves garlic

1 tablespoon peeled, minced fresh ginger

1 cup low-sodium chicken stock

½ cup fresh-squeezed, strained lemon juice

½ cup coarsely chopped, deseeded preserved lemons (about 4)

1 cup pitted dates

2 tablespoons honey

½ cup pitted black Niçoise olives

Chopped fresh cilantro, for garnish (optional)

½ cup toasted pine nuts, for garnish (optional)

Preserved lemons are salty and juicy, the perfect balance to the dates and honey in this recipe. You'll find jars of these lemons in the ethnic foods section of many supermarkets, or look for them at Mideastern markets. If you can't find Jerusalem artichokes, use new potatoes instead. I like to serve this Moroccan stew over couscous.

1. In the bottom of a slow cooker, mix together Jerusalem artichokes with half of the cumin, half of the coriander, half of the cinnamon, and half of the cayenne, plus all of the salt and pepper.

2. In a large bowl, mix together the remaining cumin, coriander, cinnamon, and cayenne with the flour. Add the chicken and coat well, shaking off and reserving the excess flour.

3. Heat the oil in a 10-inch, heavy sauté pan over medium-high heat. When the oil is hot, add half of the chicken and cook on both sides until golden brown, about 7 minutes. Place in the slow cooker on top of the Jerusalem artichokes. Repeat with the remaining chicken, about another 5 minutes.

4. Add the onions, garlic, and ginger to the hot pan, and sauté until the onions are softened, about 2 minutes. Add the reserved spiced flour and whisk until it disappears (no more than 1 minute). (Since the pan will be dry, watch carefully and keep whisking to prevent burning.) Add the stock, lemon juice, preserved lemons, dates, and honey, and raise the heat to high. Cook, whisking, until the sauce thickens, about 4 minutes. Pour over the chicken.

5. Cover the slow cooker and cook on low until the chicken is tender and cooked through, about 4 hours. Stir in the olives and ladle into individual serving bowls. Garnish with the cilantro and pine nuts and serve.

SPOTLIGHT ON

JERUSALEM ARTICHOKES

Also called sunchokes, this member of the sunflower family is a brown root vegetable resembling fresh ginger. The sweet, nutty flesh does not need to be peeled and can be cooked in myriad ways. If you can't find Jerusalem artichokes, substitute turnips, potatoes, or rutabagas. Look for firm specimens and store for up to a week in the fridge.

Vegetarian winter squash chili

SERVES 6 TO 8

One 6-inch-long by ½-inch-wide chipotle chile

1 cup low-sodium vegetable or chicken stock

½ cup dried sweetened cranberries

½ cup fresh-squeezed, strained orange juice

¼ cup tomato paste

1 tablespoon fresh-squeezed, strained lime juice

Two 15-ounce cans chickpeas, rinsed and drained

7 cups ½-inch-diced winter squash, such as butternut (about 2 small butternut squash, peeled and seeded)

2 teaspoons coarse salt

1 teaspoon ground cumin

¾ teaspoon ground cinnamon

12 grinds black pepper

1 tablespoon vegetable oil

2 cups finely chopped red onions (about 1 large)

1 tablespoon minced garlic

This fruity, spicy, easy-to-prepare chili makes an ideal vegetarian entrée for Thanksgiving. Its secret ingredient is dried cranberries, which add a subtle sweetness. Try serving it over polenta, topped with sour cream. If you'd like to reduce the heat, use only half of a chile.

1. Cover the chile in boiling water and soak for 30 minutes; drain. Cut open the chile and remove and discard the stem and seeds. Place the chile and next five ingredients in a blender and purée until smooth, about 30 seconds.

2. Mix the chickpeas, squash, salt, ½ teaspoon of the cumin, ¼ teaspoon of the cinnamon, and the pepper in the bottom of the slow cooker.

3. Heat the oil in a small, heavy frying pan over medium-high heat. When hot, add the onions, garlic, and remaining ½ teaspoon cumin and ½ teaspoon cinnamon, and sauté until the onions are softened, about 5 minutes. Stir into the squash-chickpea mixture. Then pour the puréed sauce on top. Cover and cook on low until the squash is tender, about 6 hours.

Cassoulet with croûtes and lemon-parsley butter

SERVES 6

1 pound sliced bacon, finely chopped

1 pound bulk fresh (raw) pork sausage (with no casing)

¼ cup plus 1 tablespoon all-purpose flour

1 teaspoon ground coriander

¼ teaspoon ground nutmeg

5 grinds black pepper

4 bone-in, skinless duck legs, fat removed (about 2 pounds)

15 sprigs fresh thyme

8 black peppercorns

3 dried bay leaves

8 whole coriander seeds

5 whole cloves

Two 15½-ounce cans white (cannellini) beans, rinsed and drained

3½ cups coarsely chopped Spanish onions (about 2)

1 cup carrots, peeled and finely chopped (about 1 large)

6 whole large cloves garlic

3 tablespoons Dijon mustard

1 cup Riesling wine (or another fruity white wine)

1 cup low-sodium chicken stock

1 tablespoon maple syrup

1 small baguette, sliced on the bias about ¼ inch thick

6 tablespoons unsalted butter, softened

2 tablespoons finely chopped, fresh flat-leaf parsley leaves

Freshly grated zest of 1 lemon

¼ teaspoon coarse salt

This cassoulet is just as delicious as the French original—though with easier-to-find ingredients. For efficiency's sake, prep the other ingredients while the bacon cooks. If you can't find fresh bulk pork sausage, purchase fresh sausage with casings and remove them yourself.

1. Place the bacon in a cold, 10-inch, heavy sauté pan and heat over medium. Cook until most of the fat renders, about 9 minutes. Raise the heat to medium high; add the sausage and cook, breaking it up with a wooden spoon, until lightly golden brown, about 9 minutes. Transfer the meat to the slow cooker (keeping the fat in the pan).

2. While the bacon and sausage are cooking, combine the flour, ground coriander, nutmeg, and pepper in a medium bowl. Dry the duck legs with a paper towel and dredge them in the flour, shaking off and reserving any excess flour. Place the thyme, peppercorns, bay leaves, coriander seeds, and cloves on a medium piece of cheesecloth, gather into a bundle, and secure with kitchen twine.

3. Add the duck legs to the hot fat in the pan and cook until golden brown on both sides, turning once, about 8 minutes total. Transfer the duck to the slow cooker, and then pour the beans on top.

4. Immediately add the onions, carrots, and garlic to the hot fat in the pan and sauté until the onions are softened, about 6 minutes. Whisk in the reserved flour and the mustard and cook until the flour is no longer visible, about 1 minute. Remove the pan from the heat and add the wine, then return the pan to the heat and raise the heat to high. Cook, whisking, for about 3 minutes. Add the stock and syrup and simmer for 2 minutes. Pour the sauce into the slow cooker and nestle in the spice bag.

5. Cover the slow cooker and cook on low until the duck is cooked through but not overcooked, about 4½ hours. (The duck meat will have fallen off the bones.) Let the cassoulet sit for a few minutes, then remove and discard the spice bag and duck bones.

6. About 15 minutes before the cassoulet is done cooking, heat the oven to 400°F. Place the baguette slices on a baking sheet and toast until golden brown, about 12 minutes. Meanwhile, in a small bowl, mix together the butter, parsley, lemon zest, and salt. When the baguette slices come out of the oven, slather each toast with the butter. Serve a few in each bowl of cassoulet.

Pork posole with lime and avocado

SERVES 8

2 dried bay leaves

6 black peppercorns

4 whole cloves

2 teaspoons coarse salt

20 grinds black pepper

1 teaspoon ground cumin

1 teaspoon dried oregano

One 4¼-pound, bone-in pork shoulder (after removing all excess fat)

2 tablespoons vegetable oil

Two 15-ounce cans white hominy, rinsed and drained

2 red onions, halved and cut into ¼-inch-thick slices

8 whole cloves garlic

1¼ cups low-sodium chicken stock

1 cup coarsely chopped husked tomatillos (about 3)

¾ cup pulp-free orange juice

½ cup fresh-squeezed, strained lime juice

¼ cup coarsely chopped canned jalapeños

3 avocados, peeled, pitted, and diced

½ cup sliced scallions (about 3 to 4)

½ cup coarsely chopped, fresh cilantro leaves

1 lime, cut into eighths

Tortilla chips

The crunch of tortilla chips contrasts perfectly with this comforting Mexican soup. In addition to the chips, serve the posole with sour cream and cheese or even pomegranate seeds. Canned hominy, a natural thickener, can be found in the Latin section of the grocery store.

The pork shoulder will fit snugly in your slow cooker; for ease, use turkey lifters to remove the meat from the insert, then remove the bones and gummy cartilage, break up the meat, and place the solids back in the slow cooker (without burning your hands).

1. Place the first three ingredients on a small piece of cheesecloth, bundle up into a "purse," and secure with a piece of kitchen twine. Place in the slow cooker.

2. Combine the next four ingredients in a small bowl. Rub the spices all over the trimmed pork. Heat the oil in a 10-inch, heavy sauté pan over medium-high heat. When the oil is hot but not smoking, add the meat and cook on the first side until golden brown, about 5 minutes. Turn over and brown the other side, about another 4 minutes. Transfer to the slow cooker, and pour the hominy on top and around it.

3. Add the onions and garlic to the hot pan, and sauté until softened, about 3 minutes. Add the stock, tomatillos, orange and lime juices, and jalapeños and raise the heat to high. Cook, whisking occasionally, for 5 minutes. Pour over the pork-hominy mixture in the slow cooker. Cover and cook on low until the pork is tender and cooked through, about 8½ hours.

4. Carefully remove the meat from the slow cooker and place on a cutting board. Remove and discard the spice bag. Discard any bones and gummy cartilage and shred the meat. Return the shredded meat to the slow cooker and mix into the liquid. Divide the stew among serving bowls, and top each portion with diced avocado, scallions, cilantro, lime, and chips. Serve.

SLOW COOKER SECRET

FLAVOR-BUILDING 101

Building flavor in the slow cooker can be a challenge. After all, during cooking, most ingredients release water, which generally doesn't evaporate in the appliance. Lots of water dilutes flavor, leading to bland fare. To avoid this fate, begin dishes with a sauce that's slightly too flavorful (see the sidebar on p. 7 for making a sauce). Since it will be diluted by the liquid released during cooking, you'll end up with something that's flavorful, but not overwhelmingly so.

To achieve an intense sauce, I rely on "power ingredients," such as tomato paste and mustard (for a complete list, see the sidebar on p. 6). I also like to start dishes by sautéing onions and browning meat (keeping it on the bone as often as possible).

To infuse dishes with flavor, I'll sometimes add cheesecloth sachets filled with spices or herbs (shown here), and then remove them after cooking.

- **PREP TIME:** About 1 hour (not including overnight soaking)
- **SLOW COOKER TIME:** About 10 hours ▪ **SALSA TIME:** About 30 minutes

Cuban-style spicy black beans with bacon, chile, and tropical fruit salsa

MAKES 5⅓ CUPS BEANS AND 3 CUPS SALSA; SERVES 4 TO 6

FOR THE BEANS

4 cups dried black beans that have been soaked overnight in lots of cold water to cover, then rinsed and drained

1 large carrot, trimmed and quartered

2 dried bay leaves

½ pound sliced bacon, coarsely chopped

2¼ cups coarsely chopped white or yellow onions (about 1)

1¼ cups coarsely chopped red bell peppers (about 1)

¾ cup coarsely chopped celery (about 2 stalks)

1 tablespoon plus 1 teaspoon finely chopped jalapeño (seeds and membranes removed)

9 whole cloves garlic

2 tablespoons tomato paste

2 teaspoons ground cumin

8 grinds black pepper

1 cup mild beer, such as Corona

4¼ cups low-sodium chicken stock

One 14-ounce can whole, peeled plum tomatoes, with juice

⅓ cup fresh-squeezed, strained orange juice

¼ cup cider vinegar

3 tablespoons fresh-squeezed, strained lime juice

2 tablespoons liquid from a can of chipotle chiles en adobo

2 to 3 teaspoons coarse salt

FOR THE SALSA

1¼ cups diced peeled mango or papaya

Scant cup diced peeled kiwi

¾ cup diced, peeled, and cored pineapple

½ cup finely chopped red onions (about ½ small)

3 tablespoons sliced trimmed scallions

2 tablespoons chopped fresh cilantro or flat-leaf parsley

2 teaspoons minced jalapeño (seeds and membranes removed)

½ teaspoon coarse salt

5 grinds black pepper

You don't need a Cinco de Mayo party to serve this flavorful, rustic duo. The beans are so versatile: They can be kept whole, mashed, or puréed and served as a soup, taco, or fajita filling or even as a side dish. Buy the beans in bulk so you can use exactly 4 cups, and plan to soak them the night before. Adding the salt at the end keeps the beans from becoming too tough.

Prepare the salsa right before serving, with the highest quality ripe fruit you can find.

MAKE THE BEANS

1. Put the soaked, rinsed, and drained beans, plus the carrots into the bottom of a slow cooker. Place the bay leaves on a small piece of cheesecloth, bundle it up, tie with a piece of kitchen twine, and nestle into the bean mixture.

2. Place the bacon in a cold, 10-inch, heavy sauté pan, and heat over medium heat. Cook, stirring occasionally with a wooden spoon, until the fat renders and the bacon becomes golden brown and a bit crisp, about 11 minutes. Pour out and discard (or reserve for another use) all but about 2 tablespoons bacon fat (keep the bacon in the pan). Add the onions, bell peppers, celery, jalapeño, garlic, tomato paste, cumin, and black pepper and sauté, stirring, until the onions are softened, about 3 minutes.

3. Remove the pan from the heat, add the beer, and then return the pan to the heat and raise the heat to high. Cook, stirring, for 3 minutes. Pour over the beans in the slow cooker. Add the stock, tomatoes, orange juice, vinegar, lime juice, and chipotle liquid to the slow cooker and mix well.

4. Cover the slow cooker and cook on low until the beans are tender, about 10 hours. Remove and discard the cheesecloth bag and quartered carrots. Drain the beans, discarding the liquid (or keep it and purée it with some of the beans for black bean soup). Season the drained beans with the salt to taste.

MAKE THE SALSA

In a small to medium bowl, mix together all of the salsa ingredients.

TO SERVE

Ladle beans onto individual serving plates and add a tablespoon of salsa on top. Serve the rest of the salsa at the table if desired.

Cowboy beef and bean stew with chiles, coffee, and fried plantains

SERVES 4

¼ cup all-purpose flour

2 teaspoons coarse salt, divided

½ teaspoon ground cumin

½ teaspoon ancho chili powder

Generous 1-pound beef chuck, cut into 1½- to 2-inch cubes

½ cup vegetable oil, divided

One 15½-ounce can pinto beans, rinsed and drained

One 15½-ounce can black beans, rinsed and drained

1 white or yellow onion, halved and cut into ¼-inch-thick slices

6 whole cloves garlic

¼ cup tomato paste

2 tablespoons liquid from a can of chipotle chiles en adobo

One 14-ounce can whole plum tomatoes, with juice

¾ cup low-sodium chicken stock

½ cup brewed coffee

¼ cup pulp-free orange juice

2 dried bay leaves

3 ripe but firm plantains, trimmed, peeled, and sliced ⅓ inch thick on the bias

¾ cup sour cream, for serving

¼ cup coarsely chopped fresh cilantro leaves, for garnish

This economical-to-prepare chili has more beans than meat. A bit like a red-eye gravy, it requires brewed coffee, but any kind is fine.

1. In a medium bowl, whisk together the flour, 1 teaspoon of the salt, the cumin, and chili powder. Add the beef cubes and coat with the flour, shaking off and reserving any excess flour. Add 2 tablespoons of the oil to a 10-inch, heavy sauté pan and heat over medium-high heat. When the oil is hot but not smoking, add all of the beef and brown on both sides, about 8 minutes total. Transfer to the slow cooker. Pour the beans over the meat in the slow cooker.

2. Add the onions and garlic to the hot pan, and sauté until softened, about 2 minutes. Add the reserved seasoned flour, the tomato paste, and chipotle liquid, and whisk until the flour disappears, about 1 minute. Add the tomatoes, stock, coffee, orange juice, bay leaves, and ½ teaspoon salt. Raise the heat to high and simmer for 4 minutes. Pour over the bean-meat mixture in the slow cooker. Cover and cook on low until the meat is tender, about 7 hours. Remove and discard the bay leaves.

3. About 20 minutes before serving the stew, spread paper towels on a baking sheet. Heat the remaining 6 tablespoons oil in a 10-inch heavy sauté pan over medium-high heat. When the oil is hot but not smoking, add about half of the plantains. Sprinkle evenly with ⅛ teaspoon salt and brown on the first side, about 5 minutes. Flip over, sprinkle with another ⅛ teaspoon salt, and brown on the other side, about another 4 minutes. Transfer to the paper-towel-lined baking sheet. Repeat with the remaining plantains and remaining ¼ teaspoon salt. Ladle the stew into bowls and serve with several slices of the plantains, plus the sour cream and cilantro.

SPOTLIGHT ON

PLANTAINS

Plantains, a large, hard variety of banana popular in tropical climates (Latin America, India, and Africa), are usually available unripe (green) or ripe (yellow with dark spots). The former are mild and firm and are delicious sliced, pan-fried, and mashed. The latter are sweet and soft and are also ideal sliced and pan-fried as a flavorful and crispy side dish (drizzle them with maple syrup and get ready to swoon). To prepare them, just peel as you would a banana. If you can't find plantains, try bananas (go for bananas that are more green than yellow, so they hold up when pan-frying).

Pork loin roast with dried fruit, orange, and sage

SERVES 6 TO 8

3½ pounds boneless pork loin roast

1 cup fresh-squeezed, strained orange juice, divided

¼ cup plus 1 teaspoon Dijon mustard

2 tablespoons light brown sugar

1 teaspoon dried sage

2¼ teaspoons coarse salt

15 grinds black pepper

7 dried pears

10 dried apricots

3 tablespoons unsalted butter

3 tablespoons vegetable oil

2 large sprigs fresh sage, tied together with kitchen twine

2 cups finely chopped red onions (about 1 onion)

1 tablespoon freshly grated ginger

1 tablespoon minced garlic

3 tablespoons all-purpose flour

½ cup red wine, such as Pinot Noir

½ cup low-sodium chicken stock

This special-occasion dish is ideal for holiday celebrations as an alternative to the typical turkey or beef roast. Purchase sulfured dried fruit for a prettier color, and feel free to substitute pear or apricot nectar for the orange juice. You can also opt for a white wine, such as a Riesling, rather than red. Since pork loin roast is an already-tender, lean cut, be careful not to overcook it; if you do, it will become tough.

1. Using a sharp knife, slice through the pork horizontally to form a pocket, not cutting all the way to the end (leave a 1-inch section uncut).

2. In a small bowl, mix together ¼ cup each of the orange juice and mustard, 1 tablespoon of the brown sugar, and the sage. Spread this mixture evenly all over the inside and outside of the pork. Sprinkle the inside and outside of the pork evenly with 2 teaspoons of the salt and all of the pepper. Evenly place the dried fruits inside the pork, then use kitchen twine to tie up the roast (with at least four horizontal ties and one long vertical one) to keep the pork closed and the filling inside (see the sidebar on p. 38).

3. Heat 1 tablespoon each of the butter and oil in a 12-inch, heavy sauté pan (that fits the meat) over medium-high heat. When hot but not smoking, add the pork

continued

and cook until golden brown on both sides, turning over halfway through, about 10 minutes total (you'll probably need to add 2 tablespoons more oil during this process to keep the pan lubricated). Transfer the pork to the slow cooker (cutting off any burnt kitchen twine), and nestle in the sage bundle.

4. Since your saute pan will likely have some burned bits, don't use it; instead, heat the remaining 2 tablespoons butter in a 10-inch, heavy frying pan over medium-high heat. When melted, add the onions, ginger, and garlic and sauté until the onions have softened, about 3 minutes. Stir in the flour and cook until it's no longer visible, no more than 1 minute. Remove the pan from the heat and add the wine. Return the pan to the heat and raise the heat to high. Boil the mixture for 2 minutes, stirring, until the sauce thickens and most of the alcohol cooks off. Stir in the remaining $\frac{2}{3}$ cup orange juice, remaining 1 tablespoon brown sugar, remaining 1 teaspoon mustard, remaining $\frac{1}{4}$ teaspoon salt, and stock. Pour over the meat in the slow cooker, covering it. Cover and cook on low just until tender, about 4 hours (check after $3\frac{1}{2}$ hours, as you don't want the lean meat to overcook and be tough). Cut off the twine and slice the meat, serving it with the cooking juices.

SLOW COOKER SECRET

STUFFING AND TYING MEATS

To dress up large cuts of meat, stuff and tie them prior to slow cooking. To do this, first use a sharp boning knife to trim the meat well (to remove excess fat). Then, cut the meat in half (stopping about an inch before reaching the end). Open up like a book, and stuff with flavorful ingredients, such as herbs or dried fruit. Use kitchen twine to securely close the meat over the stuffing. This will give the roast a more consistent shape, so it will not only look more attractive but also cook more evenly.

Chicken salad with Meyer lemon, tarragon, and chives

SERVES 4

2 dried bay leaves

5 whole black peppercorns

5 whole cloves

One 3½-pound whole chicken, butterflied and pressed flat (skin and bones left on)

3¾ cups low-sodium chicken stock or water

⅓ cup fresh-squeezed, strained lemon juice, preferably from Meyer lemons

1 large carrot, peeled and cut into eighths

2 stalks celery, each cut into 4 pieces, plus another ⅔ cup finely chopped

1 red onion, peeled and cut into sixths

Small bunch fresh thyme sprigs, tied with kitchen twine

1½ teaspoons coarse salt

⅔ cup minced fresh chives

¼ cup minced shallots

¼ cup mayonnaise

1 tablespoon plus 1 teaspoon freshly grated Meyer lemon zest (about 3 Meyer lemons)

1 tablespoon minced fresh tarragon leaves

1 teaspoon Dijon mustard

5 grinds black pepper

Toss some lettuce and diced apples with a mustard vinaigrette and top with a scoop of this salad. Or spoon it onto bread for flavorful chicken salad sandwiches. To butterfly the chicken, cut through the breastbone with sharp kitchen shears.

1. Place the first three ingredients onto a piece of cheesecloth; bundle up and secure with kitchen twine. Place in the slow cooker. Add the chicken, stock or water, lemon juice, carrot, 8 pieces of celery, the onions, and thyme to the slow cooker. Sprinkle with 1 teaspoon salt. Press the chicken down to submerge in the liquid.

2. Cover the slow cooker and cook on low until the chicken is cooked through, about 4 hours. Carefully remove the chicken and place on a cutting board. Remove and discard the bones and skin and chop the meat. Place the meat in a medium-size bowl. Add the remaining chopped celery, the remaining ½ teaspoon salt, the chives, shallots, mayonnaise, lemon zest, tarragon, mustard, and pepper. Mix well with a spoon and serve.

Short ribs with hoisin sauce, tangerines, and scallions

SERVES 4

6 tangerines

½ cup all-purpose flour

2 teaspoons five-spice powder

3⅔ pounds bone-in, beef chuck short ribs (about eight 3-inch-long pieces)

Scant teaspoon coarse salt

16 grinds black pepper

2 tablespoons peanut oil

1½ cups finely chopped white onions (about 1 large)

1¼ cups finely chopped peeled carrots

12 whole cloves garlic

3 tablespoons peeled, thinly sliced fresh ginger

½ cup rice wine

½ cup hoisin sauce

½ cup low-sodium chicken stock

1 tablespoon dark brown sugar

Cooked white rice, for serving

¼ cup sliced scallions (green parts only)

Plate this delicious Asian-inspired dish over white rice and serve stir-fried bok choy on the side if you like. Don't add the tangerines until right before serving.

1. With a vegetable peeler, gently peel two tangerines (avoiding the white pith) and place the peel on a medium piece of cheesecloth. Bundle up into a sachet bag and secure with a piece of kitchen twine. Place in the slow cooker.

2. Halve and squeeze the two tangerines over a strainer set over a graduated (liquid) measuring cup (you'll want ½ cup of juice). Set this juice aside. With your fingers, peel the remaining four tangerines, separating the sections and removing any obvious seeds; set the sections aside.

3. In a large bowl, mix together the flour and five-spice powder. Coat each short rib with the flour mixture, shake off (and reserve) any excess flour, and place the meat on a cutting board. Sprinkle evenly on both sides with the salt and pepper.

4. Add the oil to a 10-inch, heavy sauté pan, and set over medium-high heat. When hot, add four of the short ribs and cook until golden brown on all sides, about 10 minutes. Transfer to the bottom of the slow cooker in one layer. Repeat with the remaining short ribs, about another 7 minutes.

5. Add the onions, carrots, garlic, and ginger, and sauté, scraping the bottom of the pan with a wooden spoon, until the onions are softened, about 3 minutes. Add the reserved spiced flour and whisk until it's no longer visible, about 1 minute. Remove the pan from the heat, add the wine, put the pan back on the heat, and raise the heat to high. Cook, whisking, until the mixture is thickened, about 2 minutes. Add the reserved tangerine juice, the hoisin sauce, stock, and brown sugar, and cook, whisking, for 2 minutes. Pour over the short ribs, making sure they—and the sachet bag—are submerged.

6. Cover the slow cooker and cook on low until very tender, 7 to 8 hours. Using a large spoon or ladle, skim the fat off the surface. Remove and discard the sachet. Remove the rib bones, if desired. Stir in the reserved tangerine sections. Spoon some rice onto each plate. Top with some meat, sauce, and tangerines, then garnish with scallions.

SPOTLIGHT ON

TANGERINES

Tangerines are a type of mandarin orange with incredibly aromatic, sweet fruit and easy-to-remove peel. If you can't find tangerines, substitute clementines (another type of mandarin orange) or navel oranges. If using the latter, you won't need quite as many, since tangerines are smaller.

Beef chili with beer and lime sour cream

SERVES 8 TO 10

FOR THE CHILI

2 slices white sandwich bread

¼ cup plus 2 tablespoons whole milk

2⅓ pounds ground beef (no leaner than 85%)

2 teaspoons coarse salt

1½ teaspoons chili powder

10 grinds black pepper

2 tablespoons vegetable oil

2½ cups finely chopped white onions (about 2)

2 tablespoons minced garlic

1 teaspoon minced jalapeño

¼ cup tomato paste

3 tablespoons all-purpose flour

1 cup mild beer, such as Corona

One 14-ounce can whole peeled tomatoes

1 cup low-sodium chicken stock

One 4-ounce can fire-roasted, chopped green chiles (mild)

3 tablespoons fresh-squeezed, strained lime juice

1 tablespoon adobo sauce from a can of chipotle chiles en adobo

Two 15-ounce cans pinto beans, rinsed and drained

FOR THE LIME SOUR CREAM

2 cups sour cream

Zest of 2 limes (about 2 teaspoons)

FOR SERVING

¼ teaspoon minced jalapeño (optional)

Sour cream

Shredded Cheddar

Tortilla chips

Top this stick-to-your-ribs chili with tortilla chips, shredded Cheddar, and sliced green onions, or spoon it over tortilla chips for nachos. Feel free to use more jalapeño for spiciness. The lime sour cream is also delicious with fried plantains, eggs, and baked sweet potatoes.

MAKE THE CHILI

1. In a large bowl, mash together the bread and milk to form a paste. Add the meat, 1 teaspoon each of salt and chili powder, and the pepper. Knead well to mix.

2. Heat the oil in a medium-size saucepan over medium-high heat. When hot, add the onions, garlic, and jalapeño and sauté until the onions are softened, about 3 minutes. Add the meat-bread mixture and cook, stirring with a wooden spoon, until browned, about 8 minutes. Stir in the tomato paste and flour and cook until no flour is visible, about 1 minute.

continued

3. Remove the pan from the heat and add the beer. Return the pan to the heat and raise the heat to high. Cook, stirring, for about 2 minutes. Add the tomatoes with juices, stock, green chiles, lime juice, adobo sauce, remaining 1 teaspoon salt, and remaining ½ teaspoon chili powder. Use a potato masher to gently mash the tomatoes. Boil, stirring, for about 5 minutes. Add to the slow cooker along with the beans. Mix well, cover, and cook on low until the flavors are well melded, about 6 hours.

MAKE THE LIME SOUR CREAM
Mix the sour cream and lime zest well. Cover and refrigerate for at least 2 hours.

TO SERVE
Using a large spoon or ladle, skim the fat off the surface of the chili. Ladle chili into serving bowls and top with the lime sour cream and jalapeños at the table. Pass bowls of plain sour cream, Cheddar, and tortilla chips at the table.

SLOW COOKER SECRET

THE BEST INGREDIENTS FOR A SLOW COOKER

Perfect candidates for the slow cooker include well-muscled meats from heavily used areas of animals—think pork shoulder (called pork butt), whole or in large cubes; lamb shanks; beef brisket, chuck roast, or bottom round, whole or in cubes; veal osso bucco or breast; and poultry legs or just thighs. Lean cuts of meat (such as boneless, skinless chicken breasts) and seafood (such as salmon fillets and shrimp) can easily overcook in the slow cooker. If you use them, carefully monitor the progress of your dish.

Make sure that any large cuts of meat fit in your slow cooker. If they don't, simply cut a large portion into smaller chunks. Fat and skin will become slimy and add grease in the slow cooker, so remove all skin and all fat you can see before slow cooking.

Many hardy vegetables, including potatoes, carrots, parsnips, beets, and rutabagas, cook beautifully in the slow cooker. Eggplant and squash also thrive. Delicate vegetables and fresh herbs tend to lose their color and vibrant flavor and overcook. I'll often add these lighter-weight ingredients after cooking for contrast and punch. Meanwhile, dried herbs—especially woody, hardy ones like sage, oregano, and thyme—are ideal.

Dried beans (added after soaking), steel-cut oat groats, and arborio, instant, and converted rice also cook well in the slow cooker.

Chicken with lime, honey, and soy

SERVES 4

¼ cup plus 1 tablespoon all-purpose flour

1 teaspoon five-spice powder

1 teaspoon coarse salt

5 grinds black pepper

2½ pounds bone-in, skinless chicken thighs (about 6)

¼ cup toasted sesame oil

2 cups finely chopped red onions (about 1 large onion)

2 tablespoons thinly sliced scallions, white and light green parts only; more for garnish (optional)

1 tablespoon plus 1 teaspoon minced garlic

1 cup low-sodium chicken stock

⅓ cup honey

3 tablespoons fresh-squeezed, strained lime juice

2 tablespoons reduced-sodium soy sauce

1½-inch piece lemongrass, smashed with a chef's knife

½ teaspoon wasabi paste

2 cups cooked long-grain rice, for serving (optional)

Freshly grated lime zest, for garnish (optional)

Finely chopped, fresh cilantro leaves, for garnish (optional)

This flavorful Chinese-influenced dish is delicious served over rice and garnished with lime zest, thinly sliced scallions, and finely chopped, fresh cilantro leaves. The secret ingredients are five-spice powder and toasted sesame oil.

1. In a large bowl, mix the flour, five-spice powder, salt, and pepper. Add the chicken and coat, shaking off (and reserving) the excess flour. Heat half of the oil in a 10-inch, heavy sauté pan over medium-high heat. When hot, add half of the chicken and cook, turning over halfway through, until lightly golden brown on both sides, about 7 minutes. Place in the slow cooker. Repeat with the remaining chicken, about another 5 minutes.

2. Add the remaining oil, reserved seasoned flour, onions, scallions, and garlic to the pan. Sauté until the onions are softened, about 3 minutes. Meanwhile, in a small bowl, whisk together the remaining ingredients (except for the rice and the garnishes). Add this liquid mixture to the pan, and bring to a boil. Cook for another 5 minutes, then pour over the chicken. Cover and cook on low until the chicken is cooked through and tender, about 4 hours. Transfer the chicken to a serving platter.

3. Pour the cooking liquid into a medium-size heavy saucepan and bring to a boil over high heat. Boil until the liquid reduces by about half, about 12 minutes. Pour over the chicken and serve with rice, garnishing with zest, scallions, and cilantro, if desired.

Corned beef with Jerusalem artichokes, red potatoes, and carrots

SERVES 6 TO 8

2 pounds baby red potatoes, quartered (about 7 cups)

2 large onions, peeled and coarsely chopped

2 large carrots, trimmed, peeled, and cut into roughly 1- by 2-inch pieces

2½ cups peeled and chopped Jerusalem artichokes (cut into roughly ½-inch pieces)

½ cup drained prepared sauerkraut

2 teaspoons coarse salt

¼ cup yellow mustard; more for serving

2 tablespoons light brown sugar

One 3¾-pound beef brisket in juices, with spice packet

1 cup mild beer, such as Corona

¼ cup minced fresh chives, for garnish

8 slices rye bread, toasted, for serving

Although I rely on homemade, fresh ingredients in this book, purchasing a beef brisket in its juices with a spice packet saves a lot of time (otherwise, corned beef takes days to prepare). This entrée is like a boiled dinner: a true one-pot meal, jazzed up with sauerkraut and brown sugar. Serve the stew as is, or make sandwiches with rye bread, mustard, and pickled onions.

This recipe makes a lot of vegetables, so feel free to halve the amount, or make the full amount and fry up a hash with any leftovers and some of the corned beef.

1. Place the first six ingredients in the bottom of a slow cooker and mix well, flattening the vegetables with your hands. In a large baking dish, mix the mustard, sugar, and contents of the spice packet from the meat. Add the meat and its juices and rub the mixture all over the meat. Place the meat on top of the vegetables in the slow cooker and pour any mustard-meat-juice mix on top.

2. Pour 2 cups of water and the beer over the meat, then cover and cook on low until the meat and vegetables are tender, 10 to 11 hours. Remove the meat to a cutting board and slice it very thinly on the bias against the grain. Transfer the meat slices and vegetables to a platter, spoon some of the juices on top, garnish with the chives, and serve, passing mustard and toasted rye bread at the table.

Curry beef and pineapple stew

SERVES 6 TO 8

Scant 3 cups quartered red potatoes

2¾ pounds beef chuck, cut into 1½- to 2-inch cubes

⅓ cup all-purpose flour

¼ cup peanut oil

Heaping ½ cup coarsely chopped shallots

One 13½-ounce can light coconut milk

½ cup fresh-squeezed, strained lime juice

½ cup low-sodium chicken stock

One 6.8-ounce jar yellow curry paste (about 9 tablespoons)

3 tablespoons dark brown sugar

2 tablespoons fish sauce

4 cups 1½-inch chunks peeled and cored pineapple (about 1 small)

1 cup toasted unsalted peanuts

Chopped fresh cilantro, for garnish (optional)

3 scallions, white and light green parts, thinly sliced, for garnish (optional)

This Thai-inspired stew is perfect served over rice noodles or white or brown rice. Since this recipe relies on bottled yellow curry paste, taste it to gauge for its spiciness and saltiness. I used a salty brand, hence the absence of salt in this recipe (if the brand you buy is less salty, you might need to add a bit of salt).

1. Pour the potatoes into the slow cooker. In a large bowl, coat the beef in the flour, shaking off and reserving any excess. Heat half of the oil in a 10-inch, heavy sauté pan over medium-high heat. When hot, add half of the beef and cook until golden brown, about 7 minutes. Add another 1 tablespoon of oil and the remaining beef and repeat, about another 5 minutes. Transfer to the slow cooker.

2. Add the remaining oil plus the shallots to the hot pan, and sauté until slightly softened, about 2 minutes, scraping the bottom of the pan with a wooden spoon. Add the reserved flour, and cook, stirring, until it's no longer visible, about 30 seconds. Add the coconut milk, lime juice, stock, curry paste, brown sugar, and fish sauce, and raise the heat to high. Cook, whisking, until the sauce comes to a strong simmer, about 6 minutes. Pour over the meat and potatoes, submerging them in the liquid.

3. Cover the slow cooker and cook on low until the meat and potatoes are tender and cooked through, about 7½ hours. Let sit for 5 minutes with the lid off, then use a large spoon or ladle to skim off the surface grease.

4. Stir in the pineapple and peanuts, and serve, garnishing with the cilantro and scallions.

Curried chicken with ginger, mango, and lime

SERVES 4

3 pounds bone-in, skinless chicken thighs (about 9), excess fat trimmed

½ cup all-purpose flour

1 teaspoon curry powder

2 teaspoons coarse salt, divided

¼ teaspoon ground allspice

25 grinds black pepper, divided

3 tablespoons vegetable oil, divided

1½ cups finely chopped red bell peppers (about 1½ peppers)

1½ cups finely chopped red onions (about 1 medium)

2 tablespoons minced fresh ginger

1 tablespoon minced garlic

2 teaspoons finely chopped jalapeños (seeds and membranes removed)

1 cup low-sodium chicken stock

½ cup mango chutney, such as Geeta's

¼ cup fresh-squeezed, strained lime juice

1 tablespoon honey

1¾ cups 1-inch chunks ripe mango (about 2 large)

½ cup thinly sliced scallions, white and light green parts, for garnish

¼ cup finely chopped fresh cilantro leaves, for garnish

4 lime wedges, for serving

Inspired by Jamaican and Indian cooking, this dish brightens up long, wintry days with its tropical flavors. Be sure to purchase high-quality mango chutney, the dish's key ingredient.

1. In a large bowl, coat the chicken in the flour, shaking off and reserving the excess flour. Season the chicken on both sides with the curry, 1 teaspoon salt, the allspice, and 18 grinds of pepper. Heat 2 tablespoons oil in a 10-inch, heavy sauté pan over medium-high heat. When hot, add half of the chicken and cook, turning halfway through, until both sides are lightly golden brown, about 7 minutes. Transfer to the slow cooker. Repeat with the remaining chicken, another 4 minutes.

2. Add the remaining tablespoon oil to the pan, then sauté the bell peppers, onions, ginger, garlic, and jalapeños until the onions are softened, about 3 minutes. With a wooden spoon, add the remaining flour and stir until it disappears, no more than 1 minute. Add the stock, chutney, lime juice, honey, and remaining 1 teaspoon salt and 7 grinds pepper; bring to a boil, stirring with a whisk. Pour over the chicken. Cover and cook on low until tender and cooked through, 4 to 5 hours.

3. Just before serving, gently stir in the fresh mango. Serve, garnishing each portion with scallions, cilantro, and lime wedges.

Pot roast with root vegetables and red wine over lemony polenta with Parmigiano-Reggiano

SERVES 6

¾ cup fresh-squeezed, strained orange juice

3 tablespoons minced garlic

¼ cup plus 1 tablespoon tomato paste

1 teaspoon dried sage

One 3½-pound boneless beef chuck roast

2 teaspoons coarse salt

10 grinds black pepper

2 tablespoons unsalted butter

1½ cups finely chopped Spanish onions (about 1)

¾ cup finely chopped celery (2 to 3 stalks)

¾ cup peeled and finely chopped carrots (about 2)

¾ cup peeled and finely chopped parsnips (about 4 small)

¼ cup all-purpose flour

1 cup red wine, such as Pinot Noir

One 14-ounce can whole peeled tomatoes, with juice

¼ cup low-sodium chicken stock

1 tablespoon honey

4 sprigs fresh rosemary, tied together with kitchen twine

Lemony Polenta with Parmigiano-Reggiano (recipe on p. 52)

Like an Italian pot roast, this dish is enriched with sweet seasonal vegetables and red wine. It contrasts beautifully with tart, cheesy polenta. Try to find a chuck roast, if you can; it's fattier and more flavorful than a bottom round roast.

1. With a wooden spoon, mix together ¼ cup of the orange juice, 2 tablespoons garlic, 1 tablespoon tomato paste, and the sage. Add the meat and coat it all over with the marinade. Sprinkle evenly on all sides with the salt and pepper.

2. Meanwhile, heat the butter in a 10-inch, heavy sauté pan over medium-high heat. When melted, add the onions, celery, carrots, parsnips, and the remaining 1 tablespoon garlic and sauté, stirring occasionally, until the onions are very soft and the vegetables are starting to take on a hint of brown, about 10 minutes.

continued

3. Stir in the remaining ¼ cup of tomato paste and the flour, and cook until the flour is no longer visible, no more than 1 minute. Remove the pan from the heat and add the wine. Return the pan to the heat, and raise the heat to high. Stir until the sauce thickens, about 2 minutes. Add the tomatoes, the remaining ½ cup orange juice, the stock, honey, and rosemary, and boil for 5 minutes. Use a potato masher to gently crush the tomatoes, and stir the sauce.

4. Pour the sauce over the meat in the slow cooker, cover, and cook on low until fork-tender, about 10 hours (ideally, turn the meat over halfway through to cook it evenly). Remove and discard the rosemary, then use a large spoon or ladle to skim the fat off the surface of the sauce. Transfer the meat to a cutting board and cut off and discard the kitchen twine. Cut into chunks (the meat will be too tender to slice) and return to the sauce. Spoon the meat and sauce over the polenta.

Lemony Polenta with Parmigiano-Reggiano

SERVES 6 TO 8

½ stick unsalted butter	¾ cup freshly grated Parmigiano-Reggiano	Zest of 2 lemons
2½ teaspoons coarse salt		10 grinds black pepper
2 cups medium-grind polenta (traditional, not instant)		

Brown butter adds a deep, rich nutty flavor to this creamy side.

1. Place the butter in a small, heavy frying pan, and heat over medium heat. Cook until it melts and turns a light brown color, watching carefully, about 5 minutes. Immediately pour into a cup and set aside (the cup will quickly turn very hot).

2. In a large, heavy saucepan, bring 8 cups of cold water with the salt to a boil over high heat. Once it reaches a boil, slowly stir in the polenta and reduce the heat to low. Stir frequently for another 5 minutes, then cover the pot and let it cook until soft, another 20 to 25 minutes. Stir in the brown butter, cheese, zest, and pepper, and serve.

Dried fruit compote with Earl Grey tea and tangerine sour cream

SERVES 4 TO 6

6 to 8 tangerines

Two ½-inch cubes crystallized ginger

2 cups dried prunes

2 cups dried Turkish apricots

2 Earl Grey tea bags or sachets

¼ cup granulated sugar

1 tablespoon tapioca starch

2 tablespoons unsalted butter, cut into eight pieces

2 cups sour cream

2 tablespoons dark brown sugar

This colorful compote, subtly flavored with tea, is beautiful served in small parfait glasses. If you can't find tangerines, opt for oranges and orange juice. Drink any extra juice—your reward for being the cook!

1. With a vegetable peeler, gently remove the peel (but not the white pith) from two tangerines, and set aside. Use a Microplane zester to finely grate the zest of a third tangerine, and set aside. Squeeze these three tangerines plus the remaining tangerines over a strainer set over a liquid measuring cup; you'll need 2 cups of juice.

2. Place the peel from the first two tangerines plus the crystallized ginger on a medium piece of cheesecloth. Gather into a bundle, secure with a piece of kitchen twine, and place in the slow cooker along with the dried fruit.

3. Add the 2 cups of tangerine juice and the tea bags to a small saucepan. Bring to a simmer over medium-high heat, then cover and let sit off the heat for 10 minutes. Remove and discard the tea bags.

4. Whisk the granulated sugar and tapioca starch into the hot juice. Pour over the dried fruit-sachet mixture, sprinkle the butter over the top, cover, and cook on low until the fruit is tender, about 3 hours. Remove and discard the sachet.

5. While the fruit is cooking, whisk together the sour cream with the reserved zest and the brown sugar; cover and refrigerate until the fruit is cooked. Divide the compote among serving bowls, and spoon a dollop of the tangerine sour cream onto each portion.

Winter holiday pudding with citrus

SERVES 8

1 stick (½ cup) plus 1 tablespoon unsalted butter, at room temperature, divided

2 cups pitted, chopped dates (about 12 ounces)

½ cup sweetened dried cherries

½ cup diced candied orange peel

½ cup blanched, slivered almonds

½ cup orange liqueur, such as Triple Sec

1¼ cups all-purpose flour, divided

½ teaspoon baking soda

½ teaspoon coarse salt

½ teaspoon ground cinnamon

½ teaspoon ground cloves

¼ teaspoon ground ginger

¼ cup plus 2 tablespoons treacle or Lyle's Golden Syrup®

¼ cup plus 2 tablespoons pulp-free orange juice

1 cup packed dark brown sugar

3 large eggs

Whipped cream, sour cream, or vanilla ice cream, for serving (optional)

Moist and brown, this dessert looks and tastes like gingerbread. Serve it with brown sugar mixed into sour cream, whipped cream, or vanilla ice cream.

1. Use 1 tablespoon of butter to grease a 1½-quart oval baking dish that will fit inside your slow cooker. In a medium bowl, combine the next five ingredients and mix well. Let sit for 20 minutes, then stir in ¼ cup of flour.

2. In a medium bowl, whisk together the remaining 1 cup flour, the baking soda, salt, cinnamon, cloves, and ginger, and set aside. In a small bowl, mix together the treacle and orange juice; set aside.

3. In a stand mixer with the paddle attachment, beat the remaining 1 stick of butter and the brown sugar on medium-high speed until light, fluffy, and well blended, about 5 minutes. Add the eggs, beating well to incorporate and using a spatula to scrape down the sides of the bowl, about 1 minute. Add a third of the treacle-juice mixture, and beat on low to combine, about 5 seconds. Add a third of the flour-spice mixture, and beat on low to combine, about 5 seconds. Repeat two more times, alternating the treacle-juice and flour-spice mixtures, until just combined.

4. Pour the batter into the prepared baking dish and cover tightly with foil. Place a rack in the bottom of the slow cooker, and pour in an inch of boiling water. Add the baking dish (the water should go halfway up the sides).

5. Cover and cook the pudding on high just until a fork poked into the center comes out clean, about 3 hours. Let sit for 15 minutes before removing the dish.

Breakfast groats with mango and coconut

SERVES 8

Cooking spray

3 cups steel-cut (not whole) groats

One 33.8-ounce bottle thick mango juice drink, such as Looza (about 4⅓ cups)

Two 13.6-ounce cans light coconut milk (about 3½ cups)

1½ cups coarsely chopped sweetened dried mango slices (about 7½ oz.)

1 cup shredded sweetened coconut

2 teaspoons coarse salt

¼ teaspoon ground nutmeg

½ cup macadamias, for serving (optional)

Chopped fresh mango, for serving

Grated fresh nutmeg, for serving

Perfect when feeding a crowd, this vegan breakfast will whisk you off to the tropics in the middle of winter. Make sure to purchase steel-cut (not whole) oat groats; if you can't find them, go with steel-cut oats and cook them for less time. Both are available at natural- and gourmet-food stores. Feel free to add more coconut milk when reheating.

1. Coat the inside of the slow cooker with cooking spray. Combine all of the ingredients (other than the toppings), plus 4 cups water in the slow cooker. Cover and cook on low until tender, about 8 hours.

2. Meanwhile, toast the nuts in a dry, heavy frying pan over medium heat until golden brown, 3 to 4 minutes. Coarsely chop and set aside.

3. Ladle the cooked groats into individual serving bowls and top with the chopped nuts, chopped mango, and a pinch of nutmeg.

Citrus-lemongrass rice pudding

SERVES 6 TO 8

Cooking spray

5-inch length fresh lemongrass, finely chopped

3 cups 2% milk

3½ cups coconut milk (not low fat), well shaken (a bit less than two 13½-ounce cans)

1½ cups granulated sugar

½ teaspoon coarse salt

1½ cups uncooked medium-grain white rice, such as arborio, rinsed with cold water and drained

1½ tablespoons total freshly grated lemon, orange, and lime zest (use a mixture for the best flavor); more for serving (optional)

1 teaspoon vanilla bean paste or extract

⅛ teaspoon ground cardamom

This simple-to-prepare rice pudding—delicious served cold or warm—is creamy and perfumed with the Thai flavors of citrus and lemongrass. It's best when made with medium-grain white rice, as for risotto. Don't use long-grain or brown rice, which takes longer to cook and requires more liquid. To save time, zest the citrus with a Microplane rasp.

1. Grease the slow cooker with cooking spray. Place the lemongrass on a small piece of cheesecloth, form into a bundle, and secure tightly with kitchen twine. Add to a medium-size, heavy saucepan, along with the milk, coconut milk, sugar, and salt. Stir and bring to a strong simmer over medium-high heat (to prevent curdling, do not let boil).

2. Pour the hot mixture, including the lemongrass sachet, into the slow cooker. Add the rice and stir well. Cover and cook on low until the rice is completely tender, about 2 hours (you want there to be some liquid left). Remove from the heat, discard the lemongrass sachet, and stir in the zest, vanilla, and cardamom.

3. Let cool slightly, then pour into individual serving bowls, cover, and refrigerate until cold. If desired, garnish with additional zest before serving.

- **PREP TIME:** About 30 minutes   ▪ **SLOW COOKER TIME:** About 4 hours
- **BISCUIT AND OVEN TIME:** About 45 minutes (can occur while the filling is cooking)

Pineapple and mango cobbler with coconut biscuits

SERVES 8

FOR THE FILLING

5 tablespoons unsalted butter

Zest of 2 limes in strips, white pith removed

6 cups ½-inch diced, peeled, ripe pineapple (about 1½ pineapples, well cored)

4 cups ½-inch diced, peeled, ripe mangos (about 3½ mangos)

¼ cup treacle or Lyle's Golden Syrup

½ cup granulated sugar

¼ cup fresh-squeezed, strained lime juice

1 tablespoon rum

3 tablespoons tapioca starch

1 teaspoon vanilla extract

½ teaspoon salt

¼ teaspoon ground nutmeg

FOR THE DROP BISCUIT TOPPING

2 cups all-purpose flour

5 tablespoons plus 1 teaspoon granulated sugar, divided

3 tablespoons shredded sweetened coconut

2½ teaspoons baking powder

½ teaspoon salt

Freshly grated zest of 2 limes

1 cup plus 2 tablespoons chilled heavy cream, divided

Coconut or vanilla ice cream (optional)

If you'd like to serve this tropical dessert family-style, pour it into a 9- x 13-inch baking dish. Try it topped with coconut or vanilla ice cream.

You can make the biscuits in advance, though the dessert is most delicious when they're served warm from the oven.

PREP THE SLOW COOKER AND MAKE THE FILLING

Soften 1 tablespoon of butter and use to grease the entire inside of the crock. Place the zest in a piece of cheesecloth and tie with kitchen string. Add this bag plus the remaining butter (cut into eight pieces) and other filling ingredients to the slow cooker and gently mix with a wooden spoon. Cover and cook on low until the fruit is softened, about 4 hours.

MAKE THE DROP BISCUIT TOPPING

1. About 45 minutes before the fruit is finished, heat the oven to 400°F and line a baking sheet with parchment paper. Whisk together the dry ingredients, including the zest (with the exception of 1 teaspoon of sugar) in a medium-size bowl. Gently stir in 1 cup plus 1 tablespoon of the heavy cream. Use your hands to form a soft, relatively smooth dough, taking care not to overmix. Divide the dough into eight balls and place on the lined baking sheet. Flatten each one to the thickness of about ½ inch.

2. Pour the remaining 1 tablespoon cream into a small bowl and the remaining 1 teaspoon of sugar into another small bowl. Using a pastry brush, brush each biscuit with the cream, then sprinkle with the sugar. Bake until slightly golden and cooked through (when tested with a fork, it should come out clean), about 20 minutes. Set the biscuits aside.

TO SERVE

Remove and discard the cheesecloth bag from the slow cooker. Use a ladle to divide the fruit mixture among eight bowls and top each portion with a biscuit and a scoop of ice cream, if desired.

SLOW COOKER SECRET

SLOW COOKER SIZE AND TEMP

A key benefit of using the slow cooker is fork-tender fare, courtesy of the low-and-slow cooking process. That's why I usually cook food on the "low" setting. If you're in a rush though, you can use the "high" setting, and while the cooking process should take about half the time, it's still a good idea to check for doneness (especially on meats) before removing the insert from the slow cooker.

I developed all of the recipes in this book with a 6-quart slow cooker (which I consider to be the most versatile size), so I recommend purchasing a similarly sized appliance. Even if you're a household of one or two, going with a large model will allow you to make enough food for leftovers or guests. If you want to use a smaller-size model, try halving recipes and expect them to cook in much less time.

Meyer lemon pots de crème with Meyer lemon curd

SERVES 4

4 to 5 Meyer lemons	1 cup heavy cream	Whipped cream, for garnish (optional)
¾ cup granulated sugar, divided	⅔ cup whole milk	Sprigs of fresh mint, for garnish (optional)
8 large egg yolks, divided	1/16 teaspoon coarse salt	
1 large egg		

Each serving of this dessert contains a layer of pot de crème (pudding) on top, with Meyer lemon curd—like a surprise—on the bottom. Meyer lemon is such a special ingredient that I've let it speak for itself, not adding any other flavorings. If you have two slow cookers, use both to cook all four ramekins simultaneously. Otherwise, cook these in two batches.

Since these puddings need to chill for a few hours, I recommend preparing them a day ahead. Even if you've had a long day, delve into this recipe. You'll have a treat to look forward to the next day (and you can lick the bowl in the meantime)!

MAKE THE LEMON CURD

1. In a medium, heavy saucepan, bring about 1½ inches of water to a simmer over medium-low heat. Place a hand-held fine-mesh strainer over a medium bowl.

2. Use a Microplane rasp to zest four of the lemons (this should yield about 2 tablespoons zest). Juice two of the lemons; you should have ¼ cup plus 2 tablespoons juice. Place half of the zest, all of the juice, ½ cup of the sugar, 3 of the yolks, and the whole egg in a medium metal bowl (that can sit level atop the saucepan). Set the bowl over the simmering water (making sure that its bottom does not touch the water). Cook, whisking frequently, until the mixture thickens and can easily coat the back of a spoon, about 7 minutes (check every couple of minutes). Pour into the strainer over the bowl, using a spatula to force the mixture through. (You want to get rid of any bits of scrambled egg.) Divide the curd evenly among four 1-cup ramekins.

MAKE THE POTS DE CRÈME

Carefully wash out the saucepan, bowl, and strainer. Place the strainer over a 1-quart, glass measuring cup. Add the remaining 5 yolks to the bowl and whisk until smooth. Add the remaining ¼ cup of sugar, remaining zest, the cream, milk, and salt to the saucepan. Simmer over medium-low heat for 7 to 8 minutes, watching carefully (the mixture will thicken and small bubbles will form around the edges). Immediately and very gradually pour the cream mixture into the bowl with the yolks, whisking constantly (add slowly so as not to scramble the egg). Then pour into the strainer, pushing down on the mixture with a spatula and discarding any solids. Divide the strained liquid evenly on top of the curd in the ramekins (it should go about three-quarters of the way up the sides).

ASSEMBLE AND COOK

Cover each ramekin tightly with heavy-duty aluminum foil. Bring water to a boil in a kettle. Place two of the covered ramekins in the slow cooker. Pour the boiling water around (not on top of) the ramekins until the water reaches about halfway up their sides. Cover the slow cooker and cook on high until the custards are set (but still jiggle a tiny bit in the center), about 1½ hours. Once cooked, use tongs to carefully remove the ramekins from the slow cooker. Remove and discard the foil, let the ramekins sit at room temperature for about 15 minutes, then cover with plastic wrap. Place in the refrigerator until well chilled, about 4 to 5 hours. Repeat with the remaining two ramekins. Serve, garnishing—if desired—with whipped cream and a mint leaf.

SPOTLIGHT ON

MEYER LEMONS

Believed to be a cross between lemons and oranges, Meyer lemons are sweeter and more aromatic than traditional lemons. Their skins are thinner, and they're also rounder than their more common kin. If you can't find Meyer lemons, just opt for traditional lemons; you'll just need to add more sugar to the recipe. As when selecting any citrus, choose only unblemished fruit and store in the fridge for up to 2 weeks.

SPRING

Lamb stew with fava beans and roasted garlic served over whole wheat couscous

SERVES 6 TO 8

1 whole head garlic

7 tablespoons olive oil, divided

1 cup low-sodium chicken stock

1 tablespoon Dijon mustard

¼ cup pomegranate molasses, divided

2 tablespoons honey, divided

1 teaspoon coarse salt

10 grinds black pepper

¼ teaspoon ground cumin

¼ teaspoon ground coriander

⅛ teaspoon ground cayenne pepper

3 pounds butterflied boneless leg of lamb, well trimmed and cut into roughly 1½-inch cubes

2 large red onions, cut into ½-inch-thick rings

2 tablespoons tomato paste

3 tablespoons all-purpose flour

1 cup fruity or spicy red wine, such as Merlot or Shiraz

2 tablespoons unsalted butter

3½ pounds whole fava beans

2 cups carrots, cut into ⅓- by 1½-inch sticks (about 4)

1 cup canned chickpeas, rinsed and drained

Whole Wheat Couscous with Toasted Pine Nuts and Golden Raisins (recipe on p. 67)

In this colorful entrée, an intense sweet-and-sour sauce contrasts with the fresh, bright spring vegetables. Couscous is the perfect accompaniment: It soaks up the deep, rich, slightly spicy broth. Look for pomegranate molasses in the gourmet section at your supermarket or at Middle Eastern markets.

For ease, you can use thawed, drained frozen peas or edamame instead of the fresh favas; just stir them in at the end. And to save a bit of time, you can also purchase roasted garlic paste rather than roasting the garlic yourself. Cubed lamb shoulder meat is a good substitute for cubed boneless leg of lamb.

1. Heat the oven to 400°F. Cut the top ¼ inch off the head of garlic, then place on a piece of foil, drizzle with ½ teaspoon oil, and wrap up into a package. Roast until soft, about 1 hour. When cool enough to handle, squeeze the garlic out of the skins. Add half (1 heaping tablespoon) to a measuring cup, then whisk in the stock. In another large bowl, whisk together the remaining heaping tablespoon garlic with

continued

2 tablespoons oil, the mustard, 2 tablespoons pomegranate molasses, 2 teaspoons honey, the salt, pepper, cumin, coriander, and cayenne.

2. Add the lamb to the bowl with the mustard mixture, and mix well with your hands. Transfer the meat to the slow cooker. Add 2 tablespoons oil to a 10-inch heavy sauté pan and heat over medium high. When hot, add the onions. Sauté until they're soft and a bit golden brown, about 10 minutes (don't let them burn). Add to the slow cooker. Reduce the heat to medium and in the same sauté pan, add 2 tablespoons oil and the tomato paste and flour. Sauté until thickened, about 1 minute. Off the heat, add the wine, then return to the heat and bring to a boil over high heat. Boil for 2 minutes, then add the garlic-stock mix, the remaining 2 tablespoons pomegranate molasses, the remaining 1 tablespoon honey, and the butter. Boil, whisking often, until slightly velvety, 4 more minutes. Pour over the meat, cover, and cook on low until tender, about 6 hours.

3. Meanwhile, fill a large pot three-quarters full of heavily salted water, and bring to a boil over high heat. Next to it, place a large bowl full of salted ice water. Remove the fava beans from their pods (this should yield about 3¾ cups), then boil the beans for 1 minute. Using a slotted spoon or spider, transfer to the ice water, swish around for a minute, then drain. Remove the tender inner beans from their casings (these inner beans should be soft; yield is about 2 cups). In the same pot, boil the carrots until tender, but so they still have a slight bite, about 5 minutes. In the meantime, prepare another ice-water bath. Use a spider to transfer to the ice-water bath, then remove after a minute.

4. Use a shallow spoon or ladle to skim excess fat off the surface of the sauce. Stir the favas, carrots, and chickpeas into the meat and sauce; adjust the seasoning with salt and pepper if necessary. Serve, spooning individual portions over the couscous.

SPOTLIGHT ON

FAVA BEANS

Resembling giant lima beans, fava beans require a bit of prep. First, open up the pods and pop out the beans (discard the pods). Then blanch the beans in salted boiling water to remove their tough skins. If you're in a rush, use defrosted frozen edamame beans as a substitute.

Whole Wheat Couscous with Toasted Pine Nuts and Golden Raisins

SERVES 8

2 cups low-sodium vegetable or chicken stock

One 12-ounce box whole wheat couscous

1 cup golden raisins

⅓ cup pine nuts, tossed in a dry sauté pan over medium heat for 2 to 3 minutes

2 tablespoons unsalted butter

2 tablespoons fresh-squeezed lemon juice

2 tablespoons chopped fresh parsley leaves

2 tablespoons chopped fresh mint leaves

8 grinds black pepper

½ teaspoon coarse salt

This near-instant side offers the perfect bed for the lamb and fava bean stew.

Bring the stock to a boil over high heat in a small pot. Add the couscous to a large bowl. Pour the boiling stock over it, cover the bowl, and let sit for 8 minutes without stirring. Stir in the remaining ingredients and serve.

Chicken with white wine, wild mushrooms, and fresh herbs

SERVES 4

⅓ cup all-purpose flour

1 teaspoon coarse salt

13 grinds black pepper, divided

One 3-pound chicken, cut into eight pieces, skin removed

¼ cup unsalted butter

2 tablespoons vegetable oil

2 cups finely chopped onions (about 1 large)

2 tablespoons minced garlic

2 tablespoons Dijon mustard

2 tablespoons tomato paste

1 cup white wine, such as Fumé Blanc or Sauvignon Blanc

1 cup low-sodium chicken stock

1 tablespoon honey

1¼ pounds mushrooms, cleaned, stems removed and discarded, and caps quartered (about 5 cups)

2 tablespoons minced fresh tarragon leaves

2 tablespoons minced fresh chives

Serve tender young asparagus on the side. I also love the dish with garlic-butter-slathered baguette slices—which are ideal for soaking up the broth.

1. In a large bowl, mix together the flour, salt, and 8 grinds of pepper. Add the chicken and dredge, coating well and reserving any excess flour. Heat 1 tablespoon each of the butter and oil in a 10-inch, heavy sauté pan over medium-high heat. Once the butter has melted, add half of the chicken and cook, turning over halfway through, until lightly golden brown on both sides, about 7 minutes. Transfer to the slow cooker. Repeat with the remaining chicken and oil, about another 5 minutes.

2. Add the onions and 1 tablespoon garlic to the pan and sauté until softened, about 4 minutes. Whisk in the remaining flour, the mustard, and tomato paste, and cook until the flour disappears, about 1 minute. Take the pan off the heat and add the wine; return the pan to the heat and raise the heat to high. Cook, whisking, for about 2 minutes. Add the stock and honey and simmer for 3 minutes. Pour over the chicken, submerging the meat in the sauce. Cover the slow cooker and cook on low until the chicken is cooked through, about 4 hours. Use a ladle to skim off fat.

3. Place the remaining 3 tablespoons butter in a medium sauté pan, and heat over medium high. Once the butter has melted, add the remaining garlic, remaining pepper, and the mushrooms; sauté until the liquid disappears and the mushrooms are tender, 12 minutes. Stir the mushrooms and herbs into the chicken and serve.

Brisket sandwiches with spinach-sorrel mayo

SERVES 8

¼ cup Dijon mustard

2½ tablespoons finely chopped garlic

2 teaspoons ground paprika

4 tablespoons dark brown sugar, divided

10 grinds black pepper, divided

One 4½-pound beef brisket, trimmed if necessary and cut in half to fit into the slow cooker

2 teaspoons coarse salt, divided

2 tablespoons vegetable oil

2 red onions, halved and cut into ½-inch-thick rings

1 tablespoon tomato paste

2 tablespoons all-purpose flour

1 cup low-sodium chicken stock

Two 14½-ounce cans diced no-salt-added tomatoes, strained and juice discarded

½ cup fresh-squeezed, strained orange juice (about 2 juicy oranges)

4 cups fresh spinach leaves, torn (not packed)

2 cups fresh sorrel leaves, torn (not packed)

1½ cups mayonnaise

1 teaspoon granulated sugar

8 potato burger or brioche buns, split open and toasted if desired

Make the brisket at least a day in advance—it becomes increasingly flavorful, tender, and juicy as it sits in the sweet, tomatoey sauce. Although you can skip the flavored mayonnaise to simplify this recipe, the lemony sorrel adds a wonderful contrast to the sweet tomato sauce. If you have extra mayonnaise, use it in deviled eggs or egg salad.

1. In a small bowl, combine the mustard, garlic, paprika, 2 teaspoons of brown sugar, and 6 grinds of pepper. Place the meat on a cutting board. Use a fork to puncture it all over the surface, then slather it thoroughly with the mustard-spice mixture. Sprinkle the meat all over with about 1½ teaspoons of salt, and push it into the slow cooker.

2. Heat the oil in a 10-inch heavy sauté pan over medium-high heat. When hot but not smoking, add the onions. Sauté the onions, using a wooden spoon to scrape any brown bits from the bottom of the pan, until softened, about 4 minutes. Spoon the onions over the meat. Reduce the heat to medium and, if the pan is dry, add a tablespoon of oil. Add the tomato paste and flour. Whisk constantly until slightly thickened, about 1 minute. Add the remaining 3 tablespoons plus 1 teaspoon of

continued

brown sugar, the stock, strained diced tomatoes, and orange juice, and bring to
a boil over high heat. Boil until smooth and slightly thickened, stirring often, 2 to
3 minutes. Pour over the meat.

3. Cover and cook on low until tender, about 8 hours. Carefully transfer the meat
to a cutting board, cover with foil, and let rest for about 15 minutes. With a large
shallow spoon or ladle, skim the fat off the top of the cooking juices. Carefully pour
the juices and onions into a large, heavy pot, and boil over high heat until reduced
to a velvety sauce, skimming off any scum from the surface, about 35 minutes (this
should yield about 5½ cups). Cut the meat against the grain into roughly ½-inch-
thick slices (don't worry if it falls apart and won't slice neatly). Return the meat and
any sauce to the slow cooker, and mix.

4. Meanwhile, fill a medium-large saucepan three-quarters full of salted water,
cover, and bring to a boil over high heat. Place a large bowl of salted ice water
next to the pot. Once the water is boiling, add the spinach and sorrel and cook until
bright green and wilted, 1 to 2 minutes. Using a spider or slotted spoon, transfer to
the ice water, swish around for a minute, then drain and squeeze well with a kitchen
towel to remove all of the water (you should have a scant ½ cup of greens). Add the
greens to a food processor, along with the mayonnaise, remaining ½ teaspoon salt,
remaining 4 grinds pepper, and the granulated sugar. Purée until smooth, about
20 seconds, scraping down the sides of the bowl with a spatula. Taste, adjust the
seasoning if necessary, and set aside.

5. Place one roll on each plate and break apart. Spoon meat and sauce on one half,
slather mayonnaise on the other half, assemble, and serve.

SPOTLIGHT ON

SORREL

Imagine lemony spinach, and you have a good idea of sorrel's character. Popular
in Europe, sorrel—a hardy herb in the buckwheat family—has a short growing
season, but it is delicious, so purchase some when you find it. However, make sure
to balance its sour flavor with fat, such as mayonnaise or butter. Look for vibrantly
green (not yellow), crisp leaves; store sorrel for up to 3 days in the fridge.

Pork stew with wild mushrooms, red wine, and fresh herbs

SERVES 4 TO 6

⅔ cup (about 1 ounce) dried wild mushrooms

⅓ cup all-purpose flour

1 teaspoon coarse salt

1 teaspoon dried thyme

10 grinds black pepper, divided

2 pounds 1½-inch cubes boneless pork butt (shoulder), well trimmed

3 tablespoons unsalted butter

2 tablespoons vegetable oil

1¼ cups finely chopped peeled carrot (1 large and 1 small)

1 cup finely chopped onions (½ large)

1 tablespoon minced garlic

¼ cup tomato paste

2 tablespoons Dijon mustard

1 cup medium-bodied red wine, such as Pinot Noir

½ cup low-sodium chicken stock

2 tablespoons honey

3 cups ¼-inch diced portabella mushroom caps

2 tablespoons finely chopped fresh parsley leaves

2 tablespoons finely chopped fresh chives

1 tablespoon finely chopped fresh tarragon leaves

This earthy dish, inspired by French cooking, would be delicious over polenta. I spent less than $5 on a 1½-ounce assortment of dried wild mushrooms, and I used fresh portabella mushroom caps; however, if you feel like splurging, go for dried and fresh morels instead. Cooking the mushrooms on the stove ensures the stew won't become watery and gives the fungi the opportunity to develop a lot of flavor. Feel free to add fresh peas, if you'd like.

1. Place the mushrooms in a small bowl and pour boiling water over them to cover. Soak until soft, at least 20 minutes. Remove the rehydrated mushrooms and finely chop (you should have about ½ cup packed); set aside. Place a fine-mesh strainer (or drape a paper towel) over another small bowl. Pour the soaking liquid into it. Measure out ½ cup of this strained broth and set aside (discard the rest).

2. In a large bowl, mix together the flour, salt, thyme, and 5 grinds of pepper. Add the pork cubes and dredge well, reserving the excess seasoned flour. Heat 1 tablespoon each of the butter and oil in a 10-inch, heavy, sauté pan over medium-high heat. When hot, add about half of the meat and cook, turning over halfway through, until golden brown on each side, about 10 minutes; transfer to the slow cooker. Repeat with the remaining meat and tablespoon of oil, about another 7 minutes. Transfer to the slow cooker.

3. Immediately add the carrots, onions, and garlic to the hot pan, and sauté, stirring well, until softened, about 3 minutes. Whisk in the remaining seasoned flour, the tomato paste, and mustard, and cook until the flour disappears, no more than 1 minute. Remove the pan from the heat and add the wine; return to the heat and raise the heat to high. Simmer, whisking well to remove any brown bits from the bottom of the pan, for about 2 minutes. Add the reserved mushroom soaking liquid and reserved chopped rehydrated mushrooms, the stock, and honey, and simmer until slightly thickened, 5 to 6 minutes. Pour over the meat in the slow cooker.

4. Cover the slow cooker and cook on low until the meat is tender, about 8 hours. Meanwhile, clean the 10-inch sauté pan, add the remaining 2 tablespoons butter, and heat over medium-high heat. Once the butter melts, add the chopped fresh mushrooms and remaining 5 grinds pepper, and sauté until the mushrooms are softened and any liquid disappears, about 7 minutes. Set aside. Once the meat is cooked, stir these mushrooms as well as the fresh herbs into the stew, and serve.

SPOTLIGHT ON

MUSHROOMS

When buying fresh mushrooms, pick firm, whole fungi with tightly closed caps. Try to purchase mushrooms of the same size so they cook evenly. Store them on a sheet tray covered with a damp paper towel for up to 3 days. All mushrooms need to be cleaned well of dirt. Since they can become soggy, try to do so with a wet paper towel, or rinse them quickly under running water, but don't soak them. Even then, I recommend sautéing mushrooms prior to adding them to stews, to remove any residual water.

Of all mushrooms, morels—brown, with honeycombed, conical caps—are my favorite. Along with being gorgeous, they have a nutty, meaty flavor. To prepare morels, keep their stems and halve them vertically if they're large. If your recipe calls for a lot of morels (which are pricey and available only in spring), feel free to mix them with other varieties, such as cremini or even white button mushrooms, to cut down on cost.

Pot roast with peas and wild mushrooms

SERVES 6 TO 8

1¼ cups dried wild mushrooms (about 1¼ ounces)

One 4½-pound boneless beef chuck eye roast, trimmed if necessary

5 tablespoons minced garlic, divided

2 to 3 teaspoons coarse salt, divided

1 to 2 teaspoons freshly ground black pepper, divided

2 tablespoons vegetable oil

2 cups coarsely chopped carrots and 4 cups 1½- by ½-inch pieces carrot (about 12), divided

2 large red onions, coarsely chopped

¼ cup tomato paste

¼ cup all-purpose flour

1¼ cups dry, low-tannin red wine, such as Pinot Noir

1 small bunch fresh thyme, tied

1 to 2 pounds shelled English peas

½ stick unsalted butter, melted

¼ cup honey

Mushrooms add earthiness and complexity to this colorful pot roast jazzed up with bright vegetables. This dish makes about 9 cups of sauce; spooning some over sweet yellow polenta is ideal. You can substitute leaner bottom round roast for the beef chuck, but the fattier chuck is more tender and flavorful.

English peas, a harbinger of spring, add crisp sweetness to the finished dish (for more on peas, see p. 100). If you can't find fresh peas, go with thawed, drained frozen. For the ultimate shortcut, use a bag or two of thawed, drained frozen mixed peas and carrots instead. Or, cook the peas and carrots on the stovetop in advance and stir in at the end.

1. Put the mushrooms in a small bowl, then cover with about 2 cups of very warm water. Let sit for 30 minutes, then pour into a medium-size fine-mesh strainer set over a medium-size bowl. Reserve the mushroom liquid and finely chop the mushrooms; set aside.

2. Rub every surface of the meat with 3 tablespoons of the garlic, then sprinkle with 2 teaspoons salt and 1 teaspoon pepper. Add to the slow cooker. Heat the oil in a 10-inch, heavy sauté pan over medium-high heat. When hot but not smoking, add the coarsely chopped carrots, onions, and the remaining 2 tablespoons of garlic,

continued

and sauté until the onions are softened, about 5 minutes. Add the tomato paste and flour and cook, stirring, until thickened, about 1 minute. Off the heat, add the wine. Return to the heat, and bring the mixture to a boil over high heat, using a wooden spoon to dislodge any remaining bits from the bottom of the pan. Boil until some of the alcohol cooks off, about 2 minutes. Pour over the meat. Add 1½ cups of the mushroom broth, the chopped mushrooms, and the thyme to the slow cooker.

3. Cover and cook on low until the meat is fork-tender, 8 to 10 hours (ideally, flip the meat over halfway through to cook it evenly). Carefully transfer to a cutting board, cover with foil, and let rest for 15 minutes.

4. Meanwhile, fill a medium-large saucepan three-quarters full of water, salt generously, cover, and bring to a boil. Boil the peas until bright green and cooked through, about 3 minutes. (If using frozen peas instead of fresh, boil for 1 to 2 minutes and drain well.) Use a spider or slotted spoon to transfer the peas to a large bowl. Add the remaining 4 cups of carrots to the boiling water and cook until tender but still slightly firm, about 8 minutes, then add to the bowl with the peas.

5. Meanwhile, discard the thyme from the slow cooker. Let the sauce sit for about 5 minutes, then use a large spoon or ladle to skim off the fat. Using an immersion blender, carefully and thoroughly purée all of the sauce until smooth, about 30 seconds. Whisk in the butter and honey, and add salt and pepper to taste. Stir in the peas and carrots.

6. Remove any unpalatable membranes or twine (if the meat is tied). Slice or pull the meat apart against the grain. Add to the sauce and vegetables, and stir well. Serve.

COOKING INGREDIENTS PERFECTLY

To determine when ingredients are cooked perfectly, follow the recipe and poke and taste (without lifting the lid more than necessary). Each slow cooker cooks at a different rate, so you'll need to get to know your own appliance. Don't be intimidated: Slow cookers work at low heat, so there's little risk of burning food.

Here's what to look for when testing dishes. With meat, aim for a fork-tender texture, and use an instant-read thermometer to see if it's reached USDA-recommended temperatures (see the listing on p. 5). Sometimes, heavily muscled meat, such as beef brisket, might be cooked to the right temperature but not be fork-tender; if that's the case, re-cover the slow cooker and allow the meat to continue cooking. Brisket, as an example, usually takes about 8 hours or more on low heat to achieve the ideal texture. For already-tender meat, such as pork loin, the principle is the opposite: as soon as the meat reaches a food-safe temperature, it's done; otherwise, it will become tough and overcooked.

Hard vegetables, such as potatoes, need a long time to cook. Layer them on the bottom or along the sides of the slow cooker, and cover them with liquid. Softer, delicate vegetables, such as asparagus, can overcook or become dull in color very easily. That's why I often cook them briefly on the stovetop and stir them in after stews and other long-cooking bases have slow cooked. (If I won't be adding the vegetables until later, I'll usually blanch them in salted boiling water, shock them in salted ice water, and drain them to preserve their color.) With sturdy but not hard vegetables, like collard greens and zucchini, I'll sometimes stir them in toward the end of the slow-cooking process, re-cover the insert, raise the heat to high, and cook the dish for another 15 to 45 minutes. Very delicate greens, such as spinach, can be stirred into a hot dish and will become tender within about a minute.

With meat and produce alike, make sure that all pieces of the same ingredient are cut into roughly the same size so they cook evenly.

For desserts with biscuit or crumb toppings, I'll bake crusts in the oven to achieve a golden brown color and crisp texture, then place them atop slow-cooked fruit fillings. If you like, you can place puddings under the broiler for a few minutes after cooking to give them a golden brown topping. Just watch carefully to avoid burning.

Veal stew with asparagus, lemon, and spinach

SERVES 4 TO 6

⅓ cup all-purpose flour

1 teaspoon coarse salt, plus extra for salting the water for the asparagus

5 grinds black pepper

2 pounds 1½-inch cubes boneless veal stew meat or pork butt (shoulder), well trimmed

1 tablespoon unsalted butter

3 tablespoons vegetable oil

1 cup finely chopped onions (about ½ onion)

1 cup finely chopped peeled carrots (about 1 large)

1½ tablespoons minced garlic

1 tablespoon Dijon mustard

¾ cup crisp white wine, such as Fumé or Sauvignon Blanc

1 cup low-sodium chicken stock

¼ cup fresh-squeezed, strained lemon juice

2 tablespoons capers, drained and rinsed

2 tablespoons honey

32 stalks asparagus, ends trimmed off and cut into ½-inch slices

2 cups fresh spinach leaves (about ¼ pound if packaged), washed well

¼ cup finely chopped fresh parsley leaves

This colorful, lemon- and caper-accented dish is like a springtime stew version of veal piccata. Serve it over white rice. If you don't eat or can't find veal, substitute cubed pork shoulder (called pork butt). Regardless of what kind of meat you choose, be sure to brown it well.

A few tips for working with the vegetables: Wash the spinach until the water runs clear. There's no need to precook it, since it wilts to tenderness in the hot stew. Slice off the bottom few inches—the woody portion of the stalk—of the asparagus and discard. Then cook the trimmed asparagus on the stovetop. Doing so ensures vibrantly colored, not-overcooked, asparagus, plus it saves you time. The second the stew is cooked, stir in the vegetables, and it's ready to go.

1. In a large bowl, mix together the flour, salt, and pepper. Add the meat and dredge, reserving the excess seasoned flour. Heat the butter and 1 tablespoon of the oil in a 10-inch, heavy sauté pan over medium-high heat. When hot, add about half of the meat and cook until golden brown, turning over halfway through, about 12 minutes. Transfer to the slow cooker. Repeat with the remaining oil and meat, about another 7 minutes; transfer to the slow cooker. (Try to establish a deep golden color on the meat, but don't allow the bits in the pan to burn.)

2. Immediately add the onions, carrots, and garlic to the hot pan, and sauté until slightly softened, about 2 minutes. Whisk in the reserved seasoned flour and the mustard and cook until the flour disappears, no more than 1 minute. Remove the pan from the heat and carefully add the wine; return the pan to the heat, raise the heat to high, and simmer, whisking well, for 2 minutes. Add the stock, lemon juice, capers, and honey, and simmer, whisking well to loosen any brown bits from the bottom of the pan, about 6 minutes. Pour over the meat in the slow cooker, pushing the meat into the liquid to submerge. Cover and cook on low until the meat is tender, about 8 hours.

3. Meanwhile, fill a medium-size saucepan two-thirds full of heavily salted water and bring to a boil. Fill a large bowl with ice water and add about ½ tablespoon salt. Once the water comes to a boil, add the asparagus and cook until bright green and slightly tender, about 3 minutes. Using a slotted spoon or spider, transfer to the ice-water bath. Let sit for 2 minutes, then drain and set aside the asparagus. (You can cook and reserve the asparagus up to a day in advance of finishing the stew.)

4. Once the stew is cooked, stir in the precooked asparagus, the spinach, and parsley, and serve.

SLOW COOKER SECRET

AVOIDING OFF-FLAVORS AND TEXTURES

Food cooks for a long time in the slow cooker, so ingredients truly leave their mark! While some delicate ingredients can lose their flavor as they cook for long periods, others can almost magnify.

Although I love to use alcohol in cooking—it's ideal for deglazing bits of meat in the pan after browning—it can lend a harsh taste. So I simmer it on the stove before adding it to the slow cooker. Use a spare hand when adding salt, spicy ingredients, and soaking liquids from dried mushrooms and chiles; you can always add more later. When you peel citrus fruit for zest, make sure to remove any white pith, which can add a bitter flavor. Be sure to read the labels on packaged ingredients, looking for added salt and/or spices, which can throw off the flavor of the finished dish. For instance, purchase the Indian spice blend garam masala without salt, and avoid canned tomatoes with added basil or other flavors.

To avoid soggy, thin, bland dishes, try not to add ultra-watery ingredients, such as fresh tomatoes, cucumbers, citrus flesh, and melon. Finally, I always add a mixture of mashed up bread and milk (called a panada) to ground meat before browning; otherwise, it can become gritty in the slow cooker.

Osso buco with gremolata served over saffron risotto with English peas and spring onions

SERVES 6

FOR THE OSSO BUCO

Six 3-inch-wide, 1½-inch-high pieces bone-in veal shanks, tied (about 4 pounds; have your butcher prepare the meat for you)

1⅛ teaspoon coarse salt

¾ teaspoon freshly ground black pepper

⅓ cup all-purpose flour

¼ cup plus 1 tablespoon olive oil, divided

Zest of 1 lemon, white pith removed and discarded

3 sprigs fresh rosemary

10 sprigs fresh thyme

2 cups red onions, finely chopped (about 1)

2 cups carrots, peeled and finely chopped (about 3 large)

1 cup plus 2 tablespoons celery, finely chopped (about 2 large stalks)

4 large cloves garlic, minced (2½ tablespoons)

3 tablespoons tomato paste

1 cup dry white wine, such as Pinot Grigio

1 cup low-sodium chicken stock

One 28-ounce can whole, peeled plum tomatoes, drained

FOR THE GREMOLATA

1¼ teaspoons freshly grated lemon zest

3 tablespoons minced fresh flat-leaf parsley

1 teaspoon minced garlic

Saffron Risotto with English Peas and Spring Onions (recipe on p. 82)

The traditional Milanese duo of vibrant yellow and green risotto and flavorful, fall-off-the-bone tender osso buco is perfect for spring celebrations. The secret ingredient is tomato paste—it adds a rich intensity to the sauce. If you don't own special forks for scooping out the bone marrow, you can use knives, teaspoons, or even baby spoons.

For a more formal presentation, use kitchen twine to tie the meat to the bone (remove the twine before serving). To simplify the risotto prep, use thawed frozen peas. And, if you can't find spring onions, substitute red onions or shallots.

1. Season both sides of the veal shanks with a total of ½ teaspoon each salt and pepper, and dredge in the flour, shaking off any excess. Pour 2 tablespoons of the oil into a medium to large, heavy sauté pan and place over medium-high heat. When hot but not smoking, add four of the veal portions and brown on all sides, about 15 minutes. Transfer to a baking sheet. Repeat with the remaining two portions of veal, which should take about 10 minutes; transfer the meat to the baking sheet. If the pan becomes too dry during the browning process, add more oil, up to 5 tablespoons total.

2. Meanwhile, prepare the cooking liquid. Combine the lemon zest, rosemary, and thyme in a cheesecloth bag, and secure with kitchen string. Add the onions, carrots, celery, and garlic plus ⅛ teaspoon salt to the juices left from browning the meat, and sauté until the vegetables are a bit softened, about 3 minutes, scraping up the brown bits with a wooden spoon. Stir in the tomato paste and sauté for 1 minute.

3. Off of the heat, pour in the wine. Return the pan to the heat, and boil until reduced by a third, about 3 minutes. Add the stock and tomatoes; use a potato masher to crush the tomatoes. Boil for a couple of minutes, stirring in ½ teaspoon salt and ¼ teaspoon pepper. Add the cheesecloth bag. Carefully pour this mixture into the slow cooker. Top with the browned veal shanks (it will be a tight fit, and the veal should be about three-quarters of the way submerged in the liquid). Cover and cook on low until the veal shanks are fall-off-the-bone tender and cooked through, 6 to 7 hours (at 7 hours, the meat will separate from the bone and will be unbelievably tender and delicious).

4. Transfer the meat and bones to a baking sheet. Cut off any kitchen string, and cover with foil to keep warm. Remove the cheesecloth bag. Using a large, shallow spoon, remove some of the fat from the surface of the sauce. Then pour the juices from the slow cooker into a large, wide saucepan, and boil over high heat until reduced by half to two-thirds, about 30 minutes. Stir in ⅛ teaspoon salt and taste; adjust the seasoning again, if necessary. Remove the pot from the heat and stir in the meat and bones.

5. Prepare the gremolata by stirring together the zest, parsley, and garlic.

6. To serve, divide the warm risotto (recipe on p. 82) among six bowls, and top with the meat and sauce mixture, making sure each serving includes some bone. Sprinkle each portion with about ½ teaspoon of the gremolata.

continued

Saffron Risotto with English Peas and Spring Onions

SERVES 6

Scant 1 cup shelled English peas (about 12 ounces peas in the pod)

½ teaspoon saffron threads

1 cup dry white wine (the same wine used for the osso buco)

About 5½ cups low-sodium vegetable or chicken stock

½ stick unsalted butter, divided

1 cup finely chopped spring onions (about 2, white parts only)

1 teaspoon coarse salt

⅓ teaspoon freshly ground black pepper

1½ cups risotto rice, such as Arborio

2 teaspoons freshly grated lemon zest

1 cup minus 2 tablespoons freshly grated Parmigiano-Reggiano

1 tablespoon minced fresh chives

BLANCH THE PEAS
Fill a medium-size bowl with heavily salted ice water. Fill a small saucepan with salted water and bring to a boil. Boil the peas until bright green and slightly tender, about 2 minutes. Use a spider to transfer them to the ice water. After a minute, use the spider to transfer the peas to a bowl, and set aside.

MAKE THE RISOTTO
1. Crumble the saffron into a small to medium bowl and pour in the wine; set aside. Bring the stock to a simmer over medium heat in a medium-size saucepan. Once it's simmering, reduce the heat to medium low to keep warm. Meanwhile, melt 3 tablespoons of the butter in a medium to large, heavy frying pan over medium heat. Once the butter has melted, add the onions and ⅛ teaspoon each salt and pepper, and sauté until the onions are soft and aromatic, about 3 minutes. Add the rice and another ¼ teaspoon salt, and sauté for a minute. Add the wine-saffron mixture and bring to a boil over medium-high heat. Let cook for about 1 minute until the pan is almost dry. Reduce the heat to medium. In roughly ½-cup ladlefuls, begin adding the stock about every 2 minutes. Make sure that each grain of rice is constantly in contact with some liquid. Each time you add stock, let it cook off until only about 3 tablespoons of liquid remain. This process should continue for about 18 minutes more, during which time you should stir frequently, preferably with a wooden spoon.

2. Once the rice is tender (but not mushy) and there's a bit of liquid in the pan, add the peas and keep on the heat for 1 minute. Remove the pan from the heat, and add the remaining 1 tablespoon of butter, plus the zest, cheese, chives, and an additional ½ teaspoon salt and ¼ teaspoon pepper. Serve immediately with the osso buco.

Boneless leg of lamb with spring onion, mint, and currant stuffing

SERVES 8

1 cup dried currants

⅓ cup plus 3 tablespoons extra-virgin olive oil, divided

2 cups spring onions, bulbs coarsely chopped (about 6)

3 tablespoons garlic, finely chopped (about 5 medium cloves), divided

2 cups whole-wheat breadcrumbs (preferably unseasoned)

1 cup fresh mint leaves (not packed), finely chopped

1 cup fresh parsley leaves (not packed), finely chopped

1¾ heaping teaspoons coarse salt, divided

18 grinds black pepper, divided

¾ teaspoon ground paprika, divided

3 tablespoons Dijon mustard

2 tablespoons fresh thyme leaves

2 tablespoons honey, divided

One 4-pound boneless leg of lamb, butterflied, well trimmed of fat, and pounded to an even thickness of about 1 inch

½ stick (¼ cup) unsalted butter

½ cup shallots, thinly sliced (about 2)

1 cup fruity or spicy red wine, such as Merlot, Shiraz, or Zinfandel

1 cup low-sodium chicken stock

With a fall-apart texture similar to ragu, this festive entrée would be ideal served over polenta or couscous, with steamed asparagus on the side. Somewhat rustic in appearance, it pays off in rich, sweet flavor. For ease, order the meat in advance and ask your butcher to prepare it for you. For added intensity, feel free to rub the meat with the mustard paste and marinate it overnight.

1. Place the currants in a small bowl and cover with hot water; let stand for 15 minutes, then strain and discard the water. Heat 2 tablespoons of oil in a 10-inch, heavy sauté pan over medium-high heat. When warm, add the onions and 2 tablespoons of the garlic, and sauté until softened and a bit golden brown, about 3 minutes. Stir in the breadcrumbs and another tablespoon of oil and sauté until aromatic and slightly toasted, about 2 minutes. Pour into a medium-size bowl, and stir in the currants, mint, parsley, ¼ teaspoon salt, 6 grinds of pepper, and ¼ teaspoon paprika. Mix well and check the seasoning of the stuffing.

continued

2. Meanwhile, in a small bowl, make the mustard paste by mixing the remaining ⅓ cup oil, the remaining 1 tablespoon garlic, the remaining ½ teaspoon paprika, the mustard, thyme, and 1 tablespoon honey.

3. Place the meat on a cutting board. Make slits all over the surface with a sharp paring knife, then rub thoroughly with the mustard paste. Sprinkle all over with a heaping 1½ teaspoons salt and about 12 grinds pepper. Mound and press the stuffing into the center of the meat, leaving a ½-inch border on all sides. From the short side, gently roll up into a tight cylinder and tie a few times with kitchen twine. You might need to tie the meat four times across and one time vertically (this process is messy). Transfer to the slow cooker and pat any remaining stuffing on top to coat (there will be a lot).

4. Heat the butter in a 10-inch, heavy sauté pan over medium high. When melted, add the shallots and sauté until softened, about 2 minutes. Remove from heat, and add the wine. Return the pan to the heat and boil over high for about 3 minutes. Add the stock and boil for 2 minutes. Stir in the remaining 1 tablespoon of honey—you should have about 2 cups of liquid; pour over the meat.

5. Cover and cook on low until tender, about 8 hours (less if you'd like to slice the meat and have it somewhat hold its shape). A few minutes after the meat has finished cooking, use a large shallow spoon to skim off surface fat. Carefully remove the twine from the meat and discard. Spoon the meat and sauce onto a deep platter and serve.

Braised Vidalia onions stuffed with pork and currants

MAKES 5 ONIONS, EACH A SMALL ENTRÉE OR LARGE SIDE DISH

5 Vidalia onions

1½ tablespoons dried currants

¼ cup port or Marsala wine

1 cup low-sodium chicken stock

3 tablespoons unsalted butter

1½ tablespoons granulated sugar

½ small roll or 1 piece white bread, torn into pieces

2 tablespoons whole or 2% milk

¾ pound uncooked sweet Italian pork sausages, casings removed and discarded (about 2½ large sausages)

¼ cup extra-virgin olive oil, divided

2 tablespoons minced garlic, divided

1 tablespoon plus ½ teaspoon finely chopped fresh sage, divided

⅛ teaspoon coarse salt; more as needed

2 grinds black pepper; more as needed

5 tablespoons plain breadcrumbs

These onions are so flavorful that you'll wish your slow cooker was twice as large so you could double this recipe! The standard 6-quart model can only accommodate five onions. Make sure to purchase fresh, uncooked sausage; if you don't eat pork, use turkey or chicken sausage. To simplify removal of the casings, cut off one end, then peel off some casing, squeezing out the meat filling.

To save time, skip straining the sauce and prepare the breadcrumbs in advance. If you can't find currants, use raisins. And feel free to substitute a smaller amount of dried sage for the fresh.

1. Add about 1 inch of water to a 10- to 12-inch sauté pan, cover, and bring to a boil. Cut off about ¼ inch from each onion's stem end (not the hairy end) and peel off the skin (don't remove the root end). Place the onions in the pan, stem side down, and boil until they're tender enough for their centers to be scooped out, 15 to 20 minutes (to test, turn one over and spear the center of its stem end with a fork). Using tongs, transfer the onions to a cutting board and let cool. With a melon baller or paring knife, scoop out the centers from the stem end, making about ⅓-cup-size cavities in each onion and keeping at least two layers, as well as the hairy part, intact. Reserve the onion you scoop out, and coarsely chop a scant half of it, to total about ¾ cup.

2. Meanwhile, place the currants in a small bowl and cover with the wine; soak for 15 minutes, then drain, reserving the wine. Pour the wine into a small, heavy

continued

saucepan, add the stock, butter, and sugar, and boil over medium-high heat until slightly reduced, 5 to 10 minutes. Pour this liquid into the slow cooker.

3. Add the bread and milk to a medium bowl and mash into a paste. Add the meat and gently mix well.

4. Add half of the oil to a 10-inch, heavy sauté pan and heat over medium-high heat. When warm, add the reserved ¾ cup chopped onions and 1 tablespoon garlic and sauté until the garlic is aromatic, about 1 minute. Add the meat mixture and sauté until the meat is no longer pink and is slightly browned, breaking it into small clumps, about 10 minutes. Stir in the 1 tablespoon sage and the drained currants. Taste and add salt and pepper if necessary (make sure the mixture is cooked through first before tasting). Let sit off the heat until cool enough to handle. Spoon the filling into the onions—it should overflow out of each onion. Add the onions to the slow cooker, stuffing side up, and spoon some liquid on top. Cook on low until the onions are very tender but still retain their shape, about 4 hours (test with a fork).

5. Use tongs to carefully transfer the onions to a platter with sides. Use a large, shallow spoon to skim the fat off the top of the sauce in the slow cooker. Place a medium-size strainer over a medium frying pan with at least 1-inch-high sides, and pour the sauce into it. Discard the solids. Boil the liquid over high heat until reduced to a thick syrupy sauce (you should have a generous ¼ cup or so of sauce), about 15 minutes.

6. Meanwhile, heat the remaining oil in a small, nonstick sauté pan over medium-high heat. Add the remaining 1 tablespoon garlic and sauté until aromatic, about 1 minute. Add the breadcrumbs, the remaining ½ teaspoon sage, the salt, and pepper, and sauté until golden brown and slightly crisp, 1 to 2 minutes.

7. Pour the sauce over the onions, sprinkle with the breadcrumbs, and serve.

SPOTLIGHT ON

VIDALIA ONIONS

Vidalias are sweet, juicy, and large. Less pungent than other onion varieties, they can be eaten raw. Due to their high water content, they bruise easily and should be handled with care. Store them in a cool, dry place (such as the vegetable drawer in the fridge), and make sure they don't touch potatoes or each other, which could shorten their shelf life. If you can't find them, Walla Wallas are a good substitute.

Pita sandwiches with slow-cooked spiced beef and fava bean hummus

SERVES 6 TO 8

1¾ cups extra-virgin olive oil, divided

½ cup red-wine vinegar

½ cup fresh-squeezed, strained orange juice (about 2 juicy oranges)

5½ tablespoons finely chopped garlic plus 4 medium cloves, divided

2½ teaspoons ground cumin, divided

2¼ teaspoons ground coriander, divided

½ plus ¼ teaspoon ground cayenne, divided

8 grinds black pepper, divided

2 beef loin flank steaks, trimmed if necessary (3½ pounds total)

2¼ teaspoons coarse salt, divided; more as needed

2 red onions, halved and cut into ½-inch-thick rings

¼ cup tomato paste

2 tablespoons all-purpose flour

1 cup low-sodium chicken stock

2 pounds fava beans in pods, about 17 if large

1 cup canned no-salt-added chickpeas, rinsed and drained

¼ cup fresh flat-leaf parsley leaves

3 tablespoons fresh-squeezed, strained lemon juice

2 tablespoons tahini paste

8 individual pita breads

1 English cucumber, cut into small dice and seasoned with salt and pepper (optional)

3 large Roma tomatoes, cut into small dice and seasoned with salt and pepper (optional)

Inspired by Middle Eastern cuisine, these sandwiches pair tender braised meat in a spicy tomato broth with a gorgeous light green spread. I marinate the beef for nearly a full day before cooking it, but you could marinate it for far less time, though the flavor won't be as intense. For ease, stir the spices into the flour while preparing your ingredients and use store-bought hummus (just purée it with thawed and drained frozen edamame or even the cooked favas). You could even reduce the cooking juices a bit on the stovetop and serve the meat with the sauce alone. Other delicious accompaniments: tzatziki (a Greek yogurt-cucumber sauce) and pickled radishes.

1. Combine 1 cup of the oil, the vinegar, orange juice, 2½ tablespoons chopped garlic, 2 teaspoons each cumin and coriander, ½ teaspoon cayenne, and 5 grinds pepper in a large baking dish or 2-gallon zip-top bag. Add the meat, press down into the marinade, cover, and refrigerate for several hours and up to 24 hours. Remove the meat from the marinade (discard the marinade) and sprinkle the meat all over with about 2 teaspoons of salt. Starting from the short side of each piece of meat, roll up, and transfer to the slow cooker.

2. Heat 2 tablespoons oil in a 10-inch sauté pan over medium-high heat. When the pan is hot but not smoking, add the onions and 3 tablespoons chopped garlic and sauté until very soft and aromatic, stirring frequently to break up the onions and release any brown bits from the bottom of the pan, about 7 minutes (you might need to use another tablespoon oil). Do not let the garlic burn. Pour over the meat.

3. Reduce the heat to medium. Stir in another 2 tablespoons oil and the tomato paste, flour, ¼ teaspoon each cumin and coriander, and ⅛ teaspoon cayenne. Sauté until thickened, about 1 minute. Add the stock and bring to a boil over high heat, stirring well and boiling until smooth and thickened, about 2 minutes. Pour over the meat. Cover the slow cooker and cook on low until tender, about 6 hours. Turn off the heat. If you're not in a rush, let the meat sit in the juices for another hour.

4. Meanwhile, fill a large pot three-quarters full of salted water and bring to a boil over high heat. Next to it, place a large bowl full of salted ice water. Remove the fava beans from their pods (this will yield about 2 cups of beans), and then boil the beans for 1 minute. Using a slotted spoon or spider, transfer to the ice water, swish around for a minute, then drain. Remove the tender inner beans from their casings (these inner beans should be soft; you will have about 1¼ cups).

5. Add the garlic cloves to a food processor and chop until minced, 10 seconds. Add the tender inner fava beans, the chickpeas, parsley, lemon juice, tahini, ¼ teaspoon salt, 3 grinds pepper, the remaining ¼ teaspoon cumin, and the remaining ⅛ teaspoon cayenne. Purée until homogenous, scraping down the sides of the bowl to incorporate all ingredients, about 20 seconds. Add the remaining ½ cup olive oil and purée until very smooth, another 20 seconds. Taste the fava bean hummus and adjust the seasonings with salt and pepper if necessary (yield is about 2 cups).

6. Heat the oven to 300°F. Transfer the meat to a cutting board and slice very thinly against the grain (don't worry if it falls apart). With a shallow spoon or ladle, skim the fat off the sauce. Put the meat back into the slow cooker. Wrap the pitas in foil and heat in the oven for about 20 minutes.

7. Divide some meat and onions as well as the fava bean hummus between the warm pita breads. Top with the cucumbers and tomatoes (if using), and serve immediately.

Tartines with roasted garlic-white bean spread, fresh spinach, and radishes

MAKES ABOUT 7 CUPS SPREAD, ENOUGH FOR 20 SANDWICHES

1 pound dried cannellini (or Great Northern) beans

2 stalks celery, each cut in half horizontally

1 large carrot, peeled and cut in half horizontally

1 small bunch fresh thyme sprigs, tied with kitchen twine

5 whole heads garlic, top ¼ inch cut off

¼ cup plus 2 tablespoons extra-virgin olive oil, divided

¼ cup fresh-squeezed, strained lemon juice

1 tablespoon plus 1 teaspoon Dijon mustard

2 dried bay leaves

¼ cup white balsamic vinegar

2 teaspoons coarse salt

½ teaspoon lemon zest (about 1 lemon)

5 grinds black pepper, plus more for serving

⅛ teaspoon crushed red pepper flakes

Thick slices country bread, for serving

Radishes, trimmed and very thinly sliced, for serving

Fresh spinach leaves, washed well and stems removed, for serving

This colorful, healthful, inexpensive-to-prepare vegetarian dish was inspired by French *tartines*, or open-face sandwiches. Prepare this large batch of dip, and you'll have plenty to spread on small sandwiches for parties and on full-size sandwiches for lunch the next day! Be sure to plan ahead: Roast the garlic and soak the beans the night before, and begin cooking the beans the next morning. That night, spend just 30 to 40 minutes and dinner is ready. To truly expedite preparations, buy prewashed fresh spinach and use canned beans, skipping the slow cooker portion.

To customize the spread, divide it into two portions; add tuna and capers or olives to one batch and tahini to another.

A few additional tips: Wash the spinach until the water runs clear, and add the salt after the beans have cooked to make sure they don't get tough.

1. Put the beans in a large bowl, cover with water by several inches, and let soak overnight. After soaking, pour them into a large colander set in the sink. Rinse with more water, then drain. Pour the soaked, rinsed, and drained beans into the slow cooker, nestling in the celery, carrots, and thyme.

2. Heat the oven to 400°F. Place the trimmed garlic heads on a large piece of aluminum foil. Drizzle with 2 tablespoons of the oil, then wrap in the foil. Roast until very soft, 45 minutes to 1 hour. Squeeze the garlic into a ½-cup measure, discarding the skins (if there's more than ½ cup, save the remainder for another use).

3. Add ¼ cup of the roasted garlic, 7½ cups water, the lemon juice, 1 tablespoon of the mustard, and the bay leaves to the slow cooker. Cover and cook on low until the beans are tender, about 9 hours.

4. Carefully remove and discard the thyme, bay leaves, celery, and carrots, then pour the beans into a large strainer set over a larger bowl. Discard the cooking liquid. Pour the beans (about 6¼ cups) into a food processor. Add the remaining ¼ cup of roasted garlic, the remaining ¼ cup of oil, the remaining 1 teaspoon mustard, the vinegar, salt, lemon zest, black pepper, and pepper flakes. Purée until smooth and well blended, about 1 minute.

5. Meanwhile, toast the bread. Slather about ⅓ cup white bean spread on the bread, top with several slices of radish and a few spinach leaves, sprinkle on a small amount of black pepper, and serve.

Lamb shanks with rosemary and Shiraz over arugula mashed potatoes

SERVES 4 TO 6

¼ cup plus 1 tablespoon all-purpose flour

2 teaspoons coarse salt, divided

1 teaspoon dried thyme

10 grinds black pepper

4 pounds bone-in lamb shanks (about 4 pieces), trimmed of excess fat

2 tablespoons extra-virgin olive oil

6 sprigs fresh rosemary, tied together with kitchen twine

2½ cups finely chopped red onions (about 1 large)

1 cup finely chopped peeled carrots (about 1 large)

1 cup finely chopped cored fennel or celery

2 scant tablespoons minced garlic

¼ cup plus 1 tablespoon tomato paste

1 cup Shiraz or Syrah wine

1 cup low-sodium chicken stock

½ cup fresh-squeezed, strained orange juice

1 tablespoon honey

Freshly grated zest of 1 orange, for garnish

Arugula Mashed Potatoes (recipe on the facing page)

The lamb and arugula in this aromatic special-occasion dish make it redolent of spring. If you'd like to serve the meat on the bone and plan to cook it for longer than 7 hours, tie the flesh to the bone with kitchen twine after browning.

1. In a large bowl, mix together the flour with 1 teaspoon of salt, the thyme, and the pepper. Add the lamb and dredge well, shaking off and reserving the excess seasoned flour. Meanwhile, heat the oil in a 10-inch, heavy frying pan over medium-high heat. When hot, add two of the lamb shanks and cook until deeply golden brown on all sides, about 12 minutes. Transfer to the slow cooker. Add the remaining meat and repeat, about 6 minutes. Transfer to the slow cooker, fitting the shanks in as snugly as possible. Nestle in the fresh rosemary.

2. Immediately add the onions, carrots, fennel or celery, and garlic to the hot pan; sauté until the vegetables are softened, about 5 minutes. Whisk in the reserved flour and tomato paste and cook until the flour disappears, about 1 minute. Remove the pan from the heat, add the wine, and then return the pan to high heat. Simmer, whisking, for 2 minutes. Add the remaining 1 teaspoon salt, the stock, orange juice, and honey, and simmer for another 4 minutes. Pour over the meat in the slow cooker.

3. Cover and cook on low until the meat is very tender, about 7 hours. When ready to serve, transfer the meat to a cutting board. If desired, remove and discard the bones. Remove and discard the rosemary. Use a large spoon or ladle to skim any grease from the surface of the sauce. Return the meat to the sauce, mix, and serve the lamb over Arugula Mashed Potatoes, garnishing with the orange zest.

Arugula Mashed Potatoes

MAKES ABOUT 6 CUPS

8 Yukon Gold potatoes, each cut into eighths (peel left on)

1 bunch fresh arugula, stems cut off and discarded

2 whole medium-size cloves garlic

1 cup extra-virgin olive oil

1 teaspoon coarse salt, divided, plus extra for salting the potato cooking water

5 grinds black pepper

If you like, add freshly grated Parmigiano-Reggiano or pecorino to these nourishing mashed potatoes; if you do, reduce the amount of salt slightly.

1. Place the potatoes in a heavy, medium-size saucepan, cover with about 2 inches of heavily salted cold water, and bring to a boil over high heat. Once the water has come to a slow boil, cover the pot, reduce the heat to medium low, and simmer until the potatoes are very tender when pierced with a fork, roughly 10 minutes.

2. Meanwhile, fill a medium-size saucepan about two-thirds full of cold salted water and bring to a boil over high heat. Fill a medium-size bowl with salted ice water. Add the trimmed arugula to the boiling water and simmer for 1 minute. Immediately pour the arugula into a colander in the sink, drain, and transfer to the ice water. Swish for about 20 seconds, then drain. Squeeze the arugula, removing any ice and water.

3. Add the garlic to the bowl of a food processor and pulse continuously to mince it, about 5 seconds. Transfer the squeezed-out arugula to the food processor with the garlic, then add the oil, ½ teaspoon of the salt, and the pepper. Purée until smooth, about 20 seconds, and set aside.

4. Drain the potatoes and then return to the hot pot (placed on the hot, but turned-off, burner). Use a potato masher to mash the potatoes well. Pour in the herb oil and the remaining ½ teaspoon salt; stir to combine.

Chicken and white bean chili with tomatillo-radish pico de gallo

SERVES 6

FOR THE CHILI

⅓ cup all-purpose flour

1 teaspoon ground cumin

1 teaspoon ground coriander

1 teaspoon coarse salt

10 grinds black pepper

3¼ pounds bone-in, skinless chicken thighs (about 8)

2 tablespoons vegetable oil

3 dried bay leaves

1¼ cups finely chopped Anaheim chile (about 1 large), seeds and membranes removed

1 cup thinly sliced scallions, white and light green parts only (about 1 bunch)

¾ cup finely chopped green bell peppers, seeds and membranes removed (about 1 small)

½ cup finely chopped red onions (about ¼ large)

2 tablespoons minced jalapeño

1 tablespoon plus 1 teaspoon minced garlic

⅓ cup tomato paste

1 cup mild beer, like Corona

Two 14½-ounce cans fire-roasted crushed tomatoes

1 cup low-sodium chicken stock

¼ cup fresh-squeezed, strained lime juice

2 tablespoons honey

Two 15-ounce cans white beans, rinsed and drained

FOR THE TOMATILLO-RADISH PICO DE GALLO

1 cup finely chopped trimmed radishes (about 5)

1 cup finely chopped tomatillos (about 2 large), husks removed and fruits rinsed well

2 tablespoons finely chopped fresh cilantro leaves

1 tablespoon fresh-squeezed, strained lime juice

¼ teaspoon coarse salt

3 grinds black pepper

FOR SERVING

Sour cream

Diced avocado

Shredded Monterey Jack or Coteja cheese (optional)

The pico de gallo—fresh tomato salsa—adds a bracing shot of color and freshness to this healthful, comforting dish. To balance out the acidity of the tomato, lime, and tomatillo, top the chili and pico de gallo with sour cream, diced avocado, and—if desired—shredded Monterey Jack or Coteja cheese.

An Anaheim chile is a very mild, sweet, almost acid-green chile; find it next to the jalapeños at most grocery stores. If you can't find it, just use more bell pepper.

MAKE THE CHILI

1. In a large bowl, mix together the first five ingredients. Add the chicken and dredge well, shaking off and reserving the excess flour. Meanwhile, heat the oil in a 10-inch, heavy frying pan over medium-high heat. When hot, add half of the chicken and cook until golden brown on both sides, about 10 minutes. Transfer to the slow cooker. Repeat with the remaining chicken, about another 6 minutes. Transfer to the slow cooker. Nestle in the bay leaves.

2. Add the Anaheim chile, scallions, bell peppers, red onions, jalapeño, and garlic to the hot pan and sauté until softened, about 5 minutes. Whisk in the reserved flour and tomato paste, and cook until the flour disappears, no more than 1 minute. Remove the pan from the heat, add the beer, return the pan to the heat, and raise the heat to high. Simmer for 2 minutes, then stir in the canned tomatoes, stock, lime juice, and honey. Simmer for 4 minutes. Pour over the chicken in the slow cooker. Cover and cook on low until the chicken is cooked through, about 4 hours.

MAKE THE PICO DE GALLO

In a medium bowl, combine all the pico de gallo ingredients. Set aside.

FINISH THE CHILI

1. Once the chicken has cooked through, carefully remove and discard the bay leaves. If desired, remove and discard the chicken bones, and stir the meat back into the liquid. Stir in the rinsed and drained beans. If necessary, season with a bit more salt.

2. Spoon individual portions into bowls, with sour cream, avocado, cheese (if desired), and pico de gallo served at the table.

SPOTLIGHT ON

TOMATILLOS

Tomatillos resemble small green tomatoes; covered in thin, papery husks, these fruits taste like a cross between a Granny Smith apple and a lime and are most commonly used in salsa, guacamole, and salad. Look for firm tomatillos with husks that are securely in place. Place in a paper bag and store in the fridge for up to a month; before using them, remove their husks and wash them well.

Chicken and chive dumplings with asparagus

SERVES 6 TO 8

FOR THE CHICKEN

⅓ cup all-purpose flour

1 teaspoon coarse salt, divided, plus extra for salting the asparagus cooking water

¼ teaspoon paprika

10 grinds black pepper, divided

3 pounds bone-in, skinless chicken thighs (about 6)

1 tablespoon unsalted butter

1 tablespoon vegetable oil

2 cups finely chopped peeled carrots (about 2 large)

1¾ cups finely chopped red onions (about 1 large)

1½ cups finely chopped cored fennel

1 tablespoon plus 1 teaspoon minced garlic

¼ cup tomato paste

1 tablespoon Dijon mustard

1 cup dry white wine, such as Sauvignon Blanc

1 cup low-sodium chicken stock

2 teaspoons honey

1 bunch asparagus, bottom 3 inches cut off and the remainder cut into 1-inch pieces (about 1 cup)

FOR THE DUMPLINGS

1¾ cups all-purpose flour

¼ cup whole-grain corn flour (not coarse-ground cornmeal)

2 tablespoons minced fresh chives

1 tablespoon plus 1 teaspoon baking powder

1 teaspoon coarse salt

¼ teaspoon paprika

4 tablespoons cold unsalted butter, cut into 12 pieces

¾ cup 2% or whole milk

1 tablespoon minced fresh chives or finely chopped fresh tarragon leaves, for garnish

In this recipe, the bones are left on the chicken. While you can remove them for a more refined presentation, doing so is slightly messy. I recommend serving the dish as is and just telling your guests the meat is on the bone.

For the biscuit-like dumplings, make sure the butter is cold. You can prepare the dough in advance; just keep it cold in the fridge before you add it to the slow cooker.

Stir in the asparagus and garnish the chicken with the tarragon right before serving.

1. In a large bowl, whisk together the flour, ½ teaspoon of the salt, the paprika, and 5 grinds of the black pepper. Add the chicken and dredge well, shaking off and reserving any excess flour. Heat the butter and oil in a 10-inch, heavy sauté pan over medium-high heat. Once the butter has melted and is bubbling, add half of the chicken and cook until golden brown on both sides, about 10 minutes total. Transfer to the slow cooker. Repeat with the remaining chicken, about another 6 minutes; transfer to the slow cooker.

2. Add the carrots, onions, fennel, and garlic to the hot pan and sauté until softened, about 6 minutes. Whisk in the reserved seasoned flour, the tomato paste, and mustard, and cook until the flour disappears, no more than 1 minute. Remove the pan from the heat and add the wine; return to the heat and raise the heat to high. Whisk, simmering, for 2 to 3 minutes. Add the stock, honey, and remaining ½ teaspoon salt and 5 grinds pepper. Simmer for another 5 minutes. Pour over the chicken in the slow cooker to submerge. Cover the slow cooker and cook the chicken on low until cooked through, about 4 hours.

3. Meanwhile, fill a medium-size, heavy saucepan two-thirds full of heavily salted water and bring to a boil over high heat. Fill a large bowl with salted ice water and set it next to the stove. Once the water is boiling, add the asparagus and cook until it's bright green and crisp-tender, about 3 minutes. Immediately use a slotted spoon or spider to transfer the asparagus to the ice water; swish for about 20 seconds, then pour into a colander set up in the sink. Set aside the drained asparagus in the fridge.

4. Make the dumplings by whisking together the first six dumpling ingredients in a medium-size bowl. Once mixed well, add the butter and use your fingers to crumble the mixture into pea-shaped pieces. Add the milk, and use your hands to form the mixture into a relatively smooth dough (but don't overmix it). Form the dough into six evenly sized balls and flatten to roughly ½-inch-thick patties. If the chicken has already cooked for 4 hours, uncover it and add the dumpling patties evenly over the top. Re-cover, raise the heat to high, and cook until the dough is cooked through, about 1 hour (otherwise, refrigerate the raw dough until ready to use).

5. Using a large spoon, carefully remove the hot dumplings and set aside. Stir the cooked asparagus and fresh chives into the stew and pour it into a large serving bowl. Arrange the dumplings on top and serve family style.

Arroz con pollo with peas, peppers, green olives, and chorizo

SERVES 4 TO 6

8 boneless, skinless chicken thighs (scant 2 pounds)

1 teaspoon ground cumin

1 teaspoon smoked paprika

1¼ teaspoons coarse salt, divided

10 grinds black pepper, divided

¼ cup plus 1 tablespoon olive oil, divided

2 uncooked chorizo sausages (about ½ pound), casings removed and discarded

2½ cups red onions, diced (about 1)

1½ cups red bell peppers, diced (about 1)

1½ cups green bell peppers, diced (about 1)

2 tablespoons minced garlic

¼ cup tomato paste

2 tablespoons all-purpose flour

1 cup mild beer, such as Corona

⅓ cup fresh-squeezed, strained orange juice (about 1 juice orange)

3 tablespoons freshly squeezed, strained lime juice (about 1 juicy lime)

1 tablespoon liquid from a can of chipotle chiles en adobo

1 cup low-sodium chicken stock

½ teaspoon granulated sugar

2½ cups instant, long-grain white rice

1 cup coarsely chopped pimento-stuffed green olives (about 1 small jar)

1 teaspoon saffron threads, crumbled

2 pounds shelled English peas, fresh or frozen

⅔ cup coarsely chopped fresh cilantro leaves

This gorgeous dish has it all: tender chicken, salty olives, floral saffron, sweet bell peppers, and smoky chorizo. Make sure to use instant rice and raw or uncooked chorizo (Mexican, not Spanish).

1. Season the chicken all over with the cumin, paprika, 1 teaspoon of salt, and the pepper, then add to the slow cooker.

2. Add 1 tablespoon of oil to a 10-inch, heavy sauté pan, and heat over medium-high heat. When hot, add the chorizo and sear until cooked through, breaking the meat up with tongs, about 10 minutes. Transfer to a bowl and set aside in the refrigerator. Reduce the heat to medium. If the pan is dry, add 2 tablespoons oil.

continued

Add the onions, peppers, and garlic, and sauté until softened, scraping any bits of meat from the bottom of the pan, about 5 minutes. Pour over the chicken in the slow cooker. Add 2 more tablespoons oil to the pan, and stir in the tomato paste and flour. Sauté for 1 minute until all of the flour disappears. Raise the heat to medium high, slowly pour in the beer, and boil for 2 minutes, stirring until the sauce is smooth. Add the juices, chipotle liquid, stock, the remaining ¼ teaspoon salt, and the sugar, and bring to a boil over high heat. Boil until the sauce has thickened a bit, about 5 minutes.

3. Pour the sauce over the meat, cover, and cook on low until the chicken is tender, about 4 hours (but no more than 6 hours, or the chicken will overcook). Transfer the chicken to a bowl (leave all the sauce in the slow cooker), stir in the reserved cooked chorizo, and cover to keep warm. Add the rice, olives, and saffron to the slow cooker, cover, raise the heat to high, and cook until the rice is tender, about 30 minutes.

4. While the rice is cooking, prepare the peas. If using fresh peas, blanch for 2 minutes in salted boiling water and drain. If using frozen peas, defrost and drain well.

5. When the rice is done, stir in the reserved chorizo-chicken mixture, the peas, and cilantro. Stir to warm the chorizo through, then serve.

SPOTLIGHT ON

ENGLISH PEAS

If you see fresh English peas at the farmer's market, by all means buy them! Look for bright green, firm, medium-size pods. If you can, open a pod and check the peas, which should be small and similarly vibrant in color. Use them immediately (within 1 or 2 days), as the longer they sit, the more their sugars convert to starch. (English peas are also referred to as sweet peas because they're, well, sweet!) You'll need to shuck them, removing the peas from their pods, but the process is pretty quick. If you can't get your hands on fresh sweet peas, go with frozen, which are convenient and also very sweet.

Slow-cooked spinach strata with Gruyère and garlic

SERVES 8 TO 10

Cooking spray

1 large lemon, preferably organic

3¼ cups 2% milk

1 large loaf unsliced country bread (such as a miche boule), crusts cut off and bread diced into 1-inch cubes (8 cups)

5 tablespoons extra-virgin olive oil, divided

6 tablespoons finely chopped garlic (about 14 cloves, or 1 large head)

2 pounds prewashed fresh baby spinach, divided

1¾ teaspoons coarse salt, divided

4 cups shredded Gruyère (from slightly more than 1 pound), divided

1 cup grated Parmigiano-Reggiano, divided

10 large eggs

1 tablespoon Dijon mustard

½ teaspoon ground nutmeg

3 grinds black pepper

¼ cup minced fresh chives, for garnish

Like a grilled cheese casserole, this aromatic dish will please adults and kids alike. Make sure to follow the instructions on p. 204 for lining the slow cooker with heavy-duty aluminum foil; otherwise, the casserole might burn in some parts. When selecting a bread, avoid a multigrain (whose stronger flavor might overpower the other ingredients). Cubing it with a serrated knife will be easiest. Whether you use fresh (sautéed) or frozen spinach, drain it extremely well. If you use frozen spinach, mix it with a bit of salt and sautéed garlic after draining.

If you're pressed for time, opt for preshredded cheese, prepeeled garlic cloves, and a rectangular loaf of bread with a very thin crust. Cube the bread and let it sit out for a day or two to become stale, and you can skip baking it.

To make this dish a bit more hearty, feel free to add matchsticks of ham or prosciutto.

1. Heat the oven to 300°F. Line your slow cooker with foil to cover the hot spot and make it easy to remove the finished casserole (see p. 211), then grease the foil with cooking spray.

continued

2. With a vegetable peeler, gently peel the yellow zest from the lemon. Place on a small piece of cheesecloth, then use twine to create a small bag. Place the bag in a small to medium saucepan. Pour in the milk. Bring to a bare simmer over medium heat, then immediately remove the pan from the heat (you don't want to reduce the milk at all). Cover and let sit for 25 minutes. Set aside.

3. Place the bread cubes on a baking sheet and bake, shaking a few times, until dry, about 40 minutes. Set aside.

4. Line a large baking sheet with a kitchen towel. Add 2 tablespoons of oil to a large, heavy nonstick sauté pan and heat over medium-high heat. When warm, add the garlic. Sauté until soft and aromatic but not brown, about 2 minutes. Transfer 2 tablespoons to a large bowl and set aside. Immediately add another tablespoon of oil, one-third of the spinach, plus ¼ teaspoon salt to the pan. Using tongs, toss and cook until wilted, about 2 minutes. Transfer to the lined baking sheet. Repeat two more times with the oil, spinach, and salt. Place another towel on top of the spinach. After the spinach cools down a bit, gather up the towels and vigorously squeeze out all of the water (you'll probably need to do this several times). Set aside.

5. Add the bread cubes to the large bowl with the garlic and stir well with tongs. In a medium bowl, stir the cheeses together. Pour half of the bread-garlic mixture into the slow cooker, spacing it evenly. Then add half of the spinach, then a bit less than half of the cheese, spacing evenly. Repeat again with the three layers, reserving about ½ cup of cheese.

6. Discard the cheesecloth bag from the milk. In a large bowl, whisk the eggs. Pour in the lemony milk and the mustard, and stir in 1 teaspoon salt, the nutmeg, and pepper. Pour on top of the solids in the slow cooker, pressing down firmly with a spoon to submerge them in the liquid. Top with the remaining cheese.

7. Cover and cook on low until the internal temperature reaches 170°F, about 4 hours (no longer, or the strata can become rubbery or burn). Turn off the slow cooker, remove the lid, and let sit for 30 minutes. Carefully grab the foil handles to lift the strata out of the slow cooker, and place it on a cutting board. Gently peel away the foil, slice, and serve, garnished with fresh chives.

Lemony strawberry-rhubarb cobbler

SERVES 6

FOR THE FILLING

5 tablespoons unsalted butter, divided

Zest of two lemons in strips, white pith removed (about 2 tablespoons)

8 black peppercorns

11 cups hulled and halved (or quartered if very large) strawberries (about 4 pounds)

3 cups ½-inch-wide pieces rhubarb, halved if really thick (6 to 7 stalks, trimmed and leaves removed)

¼ cup fresh-squeezed, strained lemon juice

¼ cup fresh-squeezed, strained orange juice

2½ cups granulated sugar

¼ cup tapioca starch

½ teaspoon coarse salt

FOR THE DROP BISCUIT TOPPING

2 cups all-purpose flour

6 tablespoons plus 1 teaspoon granulated sugar, divided

2½ teaspoons baking powder

½ teaspoon coarse salt

2 teaspoons freshly grated lemon zest (about 1 lemon)

1 cup plus 2 tablespoons chilled heavy cream, divided

Vanilla ice cream, for serving (optional)

With this juicy, flavorful dessert (slightly spicy from the peppercorns), you get the best of all worlds: the fruit cooks slowly and develops complex flavors in the slow cooker, the lemony drop biscuits turn golden in the oven, and the juices reduce on the stovetop into a thick sauce that blankets the fruit. I loved this recipe so much that I "tested" it six times! As for my children, they coined it "rhubarb dessert" and now crave rhubarb as a result. This cobbler is especially good with vanilla ice cream.

For ease, zest the lemons before squeezing them for the juice. You can make the biscuits in advance, though the dessert is most delicious when the biscuits are served warm from the oven. Purchase the reddest rhubarb you can to yield a dessert with the most vivid color. Make sure to use the amount of fruit called for—it might seem like a large quantity, but the strawberries and rhubarb cook down a lot. If you'd like to serve the dessert family style, pour it into a 9- x 12-inch baking dish.

continued

PREP THE SLOW COOKER AND MAKE THE FILLING

Soften 1 tablespoon of butter, and use it to grease the entire inside of the slow cooker crock. Place the lemon peel and peppercorns in a cheesecloth bag and tie with kitchen string. Add this bag plus the remaining butter (cut into eight pieces) and other filling ingredients to the slow cooker, and gently mix with a wooden spoon. Cover and cook on low until the fruit is softened, about 4 hours (there will still be some liquid).

MAKE THE DROP BISCUIT TOPPING

About 45 minutes before the fruit is finished, heat the oven to 400°F, and line a baking or cookie sheet with parchment paper. Whisk together the dry drop biscuit ingredients (with the exception of 1 teaspoon of the sugar) and the lemon zest in a medium-size bowl. Gently stir in 1 cup plus 1 tablespoon of the heavy cream. Use your hands to form a soft, relatively smooth dough, taking care not to overmix. Divide the dough into six balls and place on the lined baking sheet. Flatten each one to the thickness of about ½ inch. Then pour the remaining tablespoon of cream into a small bowl and put the remaining 1 teaspoon of sugar into another small bowl. Using a pastry brush, brush each biscuit with the cream, then sprinkle with the sugar. Bake until slightly golden and cooked through (when tested with a fork, it should come out clean), 20 to 25 minutes. Set the biscuits aside.

REDUCE THE SAUCE

Once the fruit is cooked through, carefully remove the sachet. Place a large strainer over a medium to large, heavy saucepan, then—using oven mitts—pour the fruit mixture into the strainer. Set the fruit (in the strainer) aside. Boil the liquid over high heat until reduced to 3 to 3½ cups, about 20 minutes. Add the fruit to the pot with the thickened liquid, and mix.

SERVE THE COBBLER

Use a ladle to divide the fruit mixture among six bowls; top each portion with a biscuit and a scoop of vanilla ice cream, if desired.

SPOTLIGHT ON

RHUBARB

Rhubarb resembles red celery and in its raw state is very tart. A member of the buckwheat family, it needs to be washed and then cooked with sweetener to make it palatable. Look for bright, crisp stalks and fresh-looking leaves, but always remove the latter, since they can be toxic. Store rhubarb for up to 3 days in the fridge.

Greek yogurt parfaits with slow-cooked apricot preserves and toasted pistachios

SERVES 6

FOR THE PARFAITS

6 cups Greek yogurt

1½ cups Apricot Preserves (recipe on p. 109)

¾ cup shelled unsalted pistachios, tossed in a dry sauté pan with ⅛ teaspoon salt over medium heat for about 2 minutes (and chopped, if desired)

These beautiful treats are delicious for breakfast, a snack, or dessert (for the latter, use vanilla yogurt). If you've been intimidated to make your own preserves, this super-easy recipe is the perfect place to start. It requires very little active time and, since apricots have such thin skins, there's no need to peel the fruit. Since you'll have about 3½ cups of rich reddish orange preserves left over, use it as a topping for ice cream, French toast, or toast; stir it into oatmeal; or put it in pretty glass jars and offer it as gifts.

Into each of six parfait glasses or glass cups, spoon ½ cup Greek yogurt, then 2 tablespoons Apricot Preserves, then 1 tablespoon nuts. Repeat the layering and serve immediately.

continued

Apricot Preserves

2 large, juicy lemons, preferably organic

2½ pounds slightly firm fresh apricots

3½ cups granulated sugar

Pinch coarse salt

4½ tablespoons pectin powder, such as Ball® Classic Pectin (not low sugar)

Work quickly when pitting and cutting the apricots so they don't discolor. Use powdered pectin (not low sugar or liquid) and avoid boiling the preserves for more than 10 minutes (any longer and the pectin might break down). The preserves will continue to thicken until they're completely cool. If you'd like your preserves to last for up to a year, follow proper canning techniques.

1. Place a small plate in the freezer. With a vegetable peeler, gently peel the yellow zest from one of the lemons. Place on a small piece of cheesecloth and, using twine, tie into a bag. Add to the slow cooker. Squeeze ¼ cup juice from the lemons into a strainer set over a small bowl (you'll probably use about 1½ lemons); discard the solids. Add the juice to the slow cooker.

2. Use your hands to split open each apricot; discard the pit. Once you've repeated with all of the apricots, coarsely chop the pile with a chef's knife. Toss into a large bowl and use a potato masher to mash. Measure out 4 cups and add to the slow cooker, along with the sugar and salt. Stir well. Cover the slow cooker and cook the mixture on low heat for about 4 hours, until the fruit is broken down.

3. Pour into a large saucepan and bring to a boil over medium-high heat. Add the pectin and boil for about 9 minutes, stirring occasionally, until the pectin has dissolved and the preserves have thickened. Remove the pan from the heat and test whether the preserves have set by spooning a drop onto the chilled plate and tilting the plate. If the preserves are thick and run just a tiny bit, they're done; if not, boil for another minute, then retest. The goal is slightly runny preserves, which are perfect for a parfait. Using a funnel, carefully transfer the hot preserves into clean glass jars. Let them stand until cool, then place in the refrigerator. The preserves will last for 2 to 3 weeks.

Chocolate-ginger pot de crèmes with Cointreau strawberries

SERVES 4

4 large egg yolks

¼ cup plus 2 tablespoons granulated sugar, divided

2 teaspoons pure vanilla extract

¹⁄₁₆ teaspoon coarse salt

4 ounces high-quality 65% bittersweet chocolate (not unsweetened), cut into small pieces

1⅓ cups heavy cream

⅓ cup whole milk

Peel of 1 orange

2 heaping tablespoons finely chopped crystallized ginger, divided

2 cups strawberries, hulled and diced

3 tablespoons orange liqueur, such as Cointreau®

This sophisticated, not-too-sweet dessert is ideal for chocolate lovers since it boasts a high percentage of chocolate. Opt for a high-quality chocolate—I used TCHO PureNotes™ Dark "Nutty" 65% chocolate.

Follow these tips for success: Use a sharp vegetable peeler and press lightly to remove orange zest without any white pith. Don't make the strawberries more than a few hours in advance or they'll break down too much. Finally, if you have two slow cookers, you can make all four puddings simultaneously. If not, make them in two batches; since they cook quickly—in about 1½ hours—the whole process won't take too long.

1. In a medium bowl, whisk the yolks, 3 tablespoons of the sugar, the vanilla, and salt until smooth. Add the chopped chocolate to another medium bowl, and set a hand-held fine-mesh strainer on top. Add the cream, milk, orange peel, and 1 tablespoon of the ginger to a medium saucepan, and heat over medium until the mixture reaches a steady simmer and small bubbles form around the sides, about 5 minutes.

2. Immediately begin slowly pouring the milk mixture into the bowl with the yolks, whisking constantly. Then pour this hot milk-egg mix into the strainer set over the bowl with the chocolate. Discard the solids in the strainer. Whisk the hot milk-egg-chocolate mixture extremely well until smooth.

3. Pour the chocolate mixture into four 6-ounce ramekins (or heatproof white coffee cups) so they're three-quarters full. Cover each one with heavy-duty aluminum foil. (If you have to cook the puddings in two batches, store two, covered, in the refrigerator until ready to cook them.) Bring water to a boil in a kettle. Place two of the ramekins in the slow cooker and carefully pour hot water around them to come halfway up their sides. Cover the slow cooker and cook on high until the puddings are cooked through and set so that they only jiggle a tiny bit in their centers, about 1½ hours.

4. Use tongs to carefully remove the hot ramekins from the slow cooker, uncover them, and let sit at room temperature for about 15 minutes. Cover with plastic wrap and chill in the refrigerator until very cold, several hours. Repeat the process if you have to cook the puddings in two batches.

5. Meanwhile, add the remaining 3 tablespoons sugar, the remaining 1 tablespoon ginger, the strawberries, and orange liqueur to a medium bowl. Mix gently, cover with plastic wrap, and let chill in the fridge for an hour or two.

6. To serve, top each pudding with a heaping spoonful of the strawberries.

SUMMER

Braised pork shoulder soft tacos with watermelon-tomato salsa

SERVES 4 TO 6

One 3-pound, boneless pork shoulder roast, tied

1 cup fresh-squeezed, strained orange juice (about 2 or 3 large oranges)

½ cup plus ¼ cup fresh-squeezed, strained lime juice, divided (about 6 to 8 limes, or 1 pound)

¼ cup olive oil

1 large red onion, ½ coarsely chopped and ½ finely chopped

1 small bunch fresh oregano sprigs

⅓ cup coarsely chopped garlic (about 8 to 10 large cloves)

1 teaspoon paprika

1 teaspoon cumin

1½ teaspoons coarse salt, divided

10 grinds black pepper

4 cups packed diced watermelon

1 pint baby or cherry tomatoes, preferably yellow, halved

½ cup coarsely chopped fresh cilantro leaves

1 teaspoon minced jalapeño pepper

1 cup sour cream

1 tablespoon freshly grated lime zest (about 2 limes)

4 to 6 large soft corn or flour tortillas

In this healthful take on Latin American braised pork, lime and orange juices mimic the flavor of sour orange (which is common in Latin American countries but not in American markets). Yellow tomatoes add color to the watermelon salsa.

1. Place the pork, orange juice, ½ cup lime juice, the oil, coarsely chopped onions, oregano, garlic, paprika, and cumin in a gallon-size, zip-top plastic bag and marinate in the fridge for up to 24 hours. When ready to cook, add the meat and all of the marinade to the slow cooker. Sprinkle the pork and marinade all over with 1 teaspoon of the salt and the pepper. Cover and cook on low until tender, 6 to 8 hours. Carefully transfer the meat to a cutting board and, when cool enough to handle, remove and discard the netting or twine. Dice into roughly ½-inch cubes, then place back in the sauce.

2. In a large bowl, mix together the remaining chopped onions, remaining ¼ cup lime juice, remaining ½ teaspoon salt, the watermelon, tomatoes, cilantro, and jalapeño. In a small bowl, mix together the sour cream and zest. Wrap the tortillas in a clean dish towel, and microwave on high until warm, 30 to 60 seconds.

3. To serve, use a slotted spoon to drain the meat and spoon into a tortilla. Add a dollop of salsa and sour cream. Or serve at the table and let everyone help themselves.

Jambalaya with green peppers and summer squash

SERVES 8

1 tablespoon vegetable oil

1 pound fresh (raw) chorizo sausage (about 5 links), casings removed

1½ pounds bone-in, skinless chicken thighs (about 3)

2½ cups finely chopped white or yellow onions (about 1 very large)

1½ cups finely chopped celery (about 4 stalks)

1½ cups finely chopped green bell peppers, seeds and membranes removed (about 1 large)

3 tablespoons minced garlic

2 tablespoons minced jalapeño

¼ cup all-purpose flour

¼ cup tomato paste

1 cup mild beer, such as Corona, or white wine

One 28-ounce can diced tomatoes (without basil), with juice

1 cup low-sodium chicken stock, fish stock, or clam juice

1 tablespoon coarse salt

2 teaspoons dried thyme

1 teaspoon paprika

1 teaspoon dried oregano

20 grinds black pepper

1 pound extra-large raw shrimp, shelled, deveined, and tails left on

2 cups instant long-grain white rice, such as Minute®

2½ cups ¼-inch-dice unpeeled zucchini (about 1½)

3 cups ¼-inch-dice unpeeled yellow summer squash (about 2)

Finely chopped fresh flat-leaf parsley, for garnish

Thinly sliced scallions, for garnish

Tabasco green pepper hot sauce, for serving

Here's a quick, crowd-pleasing version of a traditional Cajun dish. For speed's sake, I don't begin with a classic roux (flour and butter cooked together until brown). I also don't include okra (since I'm not a fan) or filé powder (a somewhat difficult-to-find traditional thickener). To appeal to all palates, I use a fairly mild recipe, but you can serve the jambalaya with extra Tabasco green pepper hot sauce to add fire.

Follow these tips to guarantee success: Wear gloves to protect your hands when mincing the jalapeño. Be sure to use instant white rice—instant brown rice takes longer to cook. If you have more time, dry off the chicken with a paper towel and brown it after the chorizo (instead of with the chorizo; the result will be a deeper, more uniform brown color).

1. Heat the oil in a 10-inch, heavy sauté pan over medium-high heat. When hot, add the chorizo and chicken, and cook, breaking up the sausage and turning the chicken over halfway through, until all sides are golden brown, about 12 minutes. Transfer to the slow cooker. Add the onions, celery, bell peppers, garlic, and jalapeño to the hot pan (do not drain out any fat), and sauté, stirring occasionally, until softened, about 3 minutes. Whisk in the flour and tomato paste and cook until the flour seems to disappear, about a minute.

2. Remove the pan from the heat and add the beer or wine. Return it to the heat, raise the heat to high, and cook, whisking, for 2 minutes. Add the diced tomatoes, stock, salt, thyme, paprika, oregano, and black pepper, and cook at a strong simmer for about 8 minutes. Use a ladle to pour the sauce over the meat in the slow cooker. Cover and cook on low until the meat is cooked through, about 3½ hours.

3. Stir in the shrimp, rice, and both squash; cover, raise the heat to high, and cook until all ingredients are tender and cooked through, about 1 hour.

4. Spoon into shallow bowls, garnish with the parsley and scallions, and serve with hot sauce.

Summer brisket with roasted red peppers and fresh herb sauce

SERVES 6

3 red bell peppers

One 3-pound beef chuck brisket, trimmed

¼ cup Dijon mustard

¼ cup finely chopped garlic

2 teaspoons coarse salt

15 grinds black pepper

2 tablespoons unsalted butter

¼ cup tomato paste

3 tablespoons all-purpose flour

½ cup red wine, such as Cabernet Sauvignon

One 28-ounce can crushed tomatoes

½ bunch fresh thyme, tied together with kitchen twine

Fresh Herb Sauce (recipe on p. 120)

Vibrant with color, the rich red meat pairs beautifully with the fresh green sauce. For convenience, you can use store-bought roasted red peppers. As with all brisket, it's best to prepare it a day or two ahead of time so the flavors can meld and the meat can become juicier and more flavorful.

1. Place each pepper directly on the burner of your stove (if gas) or the grates of a gas grill set on high heat. Carefully turn the peppers with metal tongs until each is at least three-quarters blackened, about 15 minutes. Place on the countertop and cover with a large upside-down bowl. Let sit until cool enough to handle (about 15 minutes), then peel off the burnt skins. Remove the stems and as many of the seeds as you can without rinsing the peppers (rinsing can remove some of the flavor). Dice the flesh.

2. Rub the meat all over with the mustard and garlic, and sprinkle all over with the salt and pepper. Place in the slow cooker.

3. Heat the butter in a 10-inch, heavy sauté pan over medium heat. When melted, add the tomato paste and flour, and sauté, stirring, until no white flour is visible, about 1 minute. Move the pan off the heat and add the wine. Return to the heat, and bring to a boil over high, boiling for 3 minutes to cook off some of the alcohol. Add the diced roasted peppers and the tomatoes, and cook for 2 minutes. Pour over the meat in the slow cooker and nestle in the thyme. Cover and cook on low until tender, about 8 hours. *continued*

4. Carefully transfer the meat to a cutting board, cover with foil, and let rest for about 15 minutes. Discard the thyme. With a large shallow spoon or ladle, skim the fat off the top of the cooking juices. Cut the meat against the grain into roughly ½-inch-thick slices, mix back into the sauce, and serve, with the herb sauce drizzled on top, if desired.

Fresh Herb Sauce

MAKES ABOUT 1½ CUPS

1 cup packed fresh flat-leaf parsley leaves	1 cup coarsely chopped shallots (about 3 medium)	½ teaspoon coarse salt
1 cup packed fresh basil leaves	¼ cup plus 2 tablespoons golden or white balsamic vinegar	8 grinds black pepper
		½ cup extra-virgin olive oil

Sweet balsamic vinegar and shallots meet grassy herbs and rich oil in this simple sauce—ready in just a few seconds.

Add all of the ingredients except the oil to a food processor, and purée until finely chopped, about 25 seconds (use a small spatula to push the mixture down the sides of the bowl to evenly distribute it). With the machine running, drizzle in the oil, and purée until very smooth, another 10 to 20 seconds.

MAKING SLOW-COOKED DISHES FLAVORFUL

One of the most common ways to ensure a dish will be tasty is to reduce the ingredients' water content to concentrate flavor. Unfortunately, since the slow cooker is covered and operates at low temperatures, little—if any—of this evaporation occurs. Even more challenging, most foods emit liquid while in the slow cooker, making it easy for dishes to become watery and bland.

Fortunately, there are a few solutions.

- Use lots of high-impact ingredients in large quantities (see "Power Ingredients" on p. 6 for a list).
- Start your sauce on the stovetop and make it a bit too thick. Since it will likely thin out as other ingredients leach liquid, you'll end up with a sauce that's the ideal consistency.
- Incorporate thickeners—they're truly heroes when it comes to slow cooking! Here are just a few of the many from which to choose: flour (by itself, kneaded with butter, or cooked with fat to make a roux), tapioca starch, cornstarch, and arrowroot.

The two approaches I use most frequently in these recipes are flour cooked with fat (my favored method for savory fare) and tapioca starch—also called tapioca flour—(for desserts).

With flour, I incorporate an average of ¼ cup, which tends to be just the right amount to counteract the liquid released in dishes designed for 6-quart slow cookers. If I'm browning meat, I'll usually first coat it in seasoned flour before placing it in a hot pan, then I'll add any excess flour after I've sautéed my vegetables. Doing so not only improves the golden brown color of the meat, but also allows me to easily add my thickener. Otherwise, I'll often sauté the vegetables and then add all of the flour. In both cases, I simmer the flour, whisking it well, until it dissolves into the liquid.

In dessert recipes, I use tapioca starch, which thickens at low temperatures and—since it's finely ground—dissolves completely and quickly. You can find it at natural-food stores. If you need a substitute, try instant tapioca (which you might want to pulse in the blender to reduce it to the size of beads), arrowroot, cornstarch, or potato starch (the last two won't disappear completely or give your dish a glossy sheen). Finally, don't worry if a dessert, such as a rice pudding, seems a bit too thin: once chilled, it will likely thicken to the perfect consistency.

Philly cheesesteak sandwiches with tomato chutney

SERVES 4 TO 6

FOR THE BEEF

¼ cup finely chopped garlic, divided

2 tablespoons yellow mustard

2 tablespoons coarsely chopped capers, rinsed and drained

One 2½-pound boneless chuck eye roast, trimmed of excess fat

2 to 3 tablespoons vegetable oil

1½ large red onions, halved and cut into ¼-inch-thick rings (about 4 cups)

2 large green bell peppers, halved and cut into ¼-inch-thick rings (about 4 cups)

½ teaspoon coarse salt

10 grinds black pepper

¼ cup tomato paste

2 tablespoons all-purpose flour

1 cup low-sodium chicken stock

½ bunch fresh oregano, tied together with kitchen twine

FOR THE CHUTNEY

6 whole black peppercorns

8 whole cloves

½ teaspoon yellow mustard seeds

½ cup plus 1 tablespoon dark brown sugar

½ cup cider vinegar

3 tablespoons fresh-squeezed, strained lemon juice (about 2 lemons)

½ teaspoon ground ginger

4 cups diced fresh tomatoes (about 3 ripe tomatoes, or 2 pounds)

1 cup finely chopped red onions (about ½ red onion, left over from the meat)

½ cup golden raisins

FOR THE SANDWICHES

4 to 6 hoagie rolls, split lengthwise and toasted

8 ounces shredded Cheddar cheese

1 cup mayonnaise mixed with 2 tablespoons finely chopped garlic, seasoned if necessary

This seasonal tomato chutney provides a new spin on the Philly cheesesteak, which is traditionally slathered with marinara sauce or ketchup. In this recipe, I substitute the typical provolone or mozzarella with Cheddar.

The chutney recipe makes about 2¼ cups, so try leftovers on turkey or roast beef sandwiches. For the most refined presentation and texture, you can peel the tomatoes.

To save time, use canned tomatoes in the chutney and purchase preshredded cheese (though you'll get better flavor if you buy a chunk and grate it yourself). For the best results, prepare the steak one day ahead and let it sit in the sauce.

COOK THE BEEF

1. In a small bowl, mix together 3 tablespoons of the garlic plus the mustard and capers. Rub all over the meat and place in the slow cooker.

2. Heat the oil in a 10-inch, heavy sauté pan over medium-high heat. When the pan is hot, add the remaining 1 tablespoon garlic, the onions, bell peppers, salt, and pepper and sauté, stirring often, until very soft and aromatic, about 8 minutes. Pour half of the mixture over the meat and refrigerate the remainder for serving later.

3. Reduce the heat to medium and stir in the tomato paste and flour. Sauté, stirring with a wooden spoon, until no white flour is visible, about 1 minute (if the pan is dry, add 1 tablespoon of oil before adding the tomato paste and flour). Add the stock and bring to a boil over high heat, stirring well and cooking until smooth, about 2 minutes. Pour over the meat and nestle in the oregano. Cover the slow cooker and cook on low until tender, about 8 hours.

4. Turn off the heat. If you're not in a rush, let the meat sit in the juices for another hour. Just before serving, transfer the meat to a cutting board, slice very thinly against the grain, and place back in the meat juice.

MAKE THE CHUTNEY

Place the first three ingredients on a medium-size piece of cheesecloth. Use twine to tie up into a small bag. Place in a medium-size saucepan, along with the brown sugar, vinegar, lemon juice, and ginger. Bring to a boil over high heat, then add the tomatoes, onions, and raisins, and stir well. Reduce the heat to medium high and cook until thickened to a semithick consistency and very little liquid remains, about 40 minutes. Cool to room temperature.

ASSEMBLE THE SANDWICHES

Heat the oven to 350°F. Use a serrated knife to slice each hoagie in half, and place half of those halves on a baking sheet. Top each one with some meat and pepper-onion mixture, then shredded cheese and the remaining bread halves; wrap each sandwich in aluminum foil. Bake until the cheese melts, about 10 minutes. Remove the sandwiches from the oven, dollop about 3 tablespoons chutney and 2 tablespoons mayonnaise inside each, and serve.

Braised chicken with red peppers, olives, and raisins

SERVES 4 TO 6

8 bone-in, skinless chicken thighs, trimmed (scant 2 pounds)

¼ cup minced garlic, divided

1 teaspoon paprika

1 teaspoon coarse salt

15 grinds black pepper, divided

¼ cup unsalted butter, divided

2½ cups red onions, diced (about 1)

1½ cups red bell peppers, diced (about 1)

¼ cup tomato paste

3 tablespoons all-purpose flour

One 28-ounce can whole plum tomatoes

¼ cup plus 2 tablespoons balsamic vinegar

2 teaspoons light brown sugar

3 sprigs fresh rosemary

3 sprigs fresh oregano

1 cup pitted black olives

½ cup raisins

¼ cup capers, rinsed and drained

Serve this saucy chicken—inspired by the sweet and savory flavors of Sicilian cooking—over buttery pappardelle pasta, toasted Italian bread, or creamy sweet polenta. To make the dish dairy-free, swap olive oil for the butter.

1. Rub the chicken evenly with half of the garlic, then sprinkle evenly with paprika, salt, and 10 grinds of the pepper. Place in the slow cooker. Heat half of the butter in a 10-inch, heavy sauté pan over medium-high heat. When melted, add the onions, bell peppers, and remaining garlic, and sauté until softened, about 8 minutes. Transfer to the slow cooker. Reduce the heat to medium and add the remaining butter; once it melts, stir in the tomato paste and flour, and cook, stirring, until the flour is no longer visible, about 1 minute. Add the tomatoes, vinegar, brown sugar, and remaining 5 grinds pepper. Boil over high heat for about 3 minutes, stirring, until relatively smooth; pour over the chicken. Use kitchen twine to tie together the herb sprigs, then nestle into the sauce.

2. Cover and cook on low until the chicken is tender and cooked through, about 4 hours. Remove the herbs from the slow cooker and discard. Let the chicken sit for 5 minutes, then use a large shallow spoon to degrease the sauce. Stir in the olives, raisins, and capers, and serve.

Braised Turkish eggplant with cucumber tzatziki

SERVES 6

13 cups ½-inch-dice eggplant (about 3 large)

2 tablespoons olive oil

2½ cups finely chopped green bell peppers (about 2½)

2½ cups finely chopped yellow or white onions (about 1¼ large)

¼ cup thinly sliced scallions, white and light green parts only (1 to 2)

12 whole cloves garlic

2½ teaspoons coarse salt

1 teaspoon dried oregano

1 teaspoon dried dill

¼ teaspoon ground cinnamon

¼ teaspoon crushed red pepper flakes

10 grinds black pepper

¼ cup tomato paste

¼ cup all-purpose flour

One 28-ounce can whole peeled tomatoes

¼ cup fresh-squeezed, strained lemon juice

3 tablespoons honey

Couscous, for serving (optional)

Cucumber Tzatziki (recipe on the facing page)

This dish is delicious served over couscous with chickpeas and fresh herbs (such as dill, mint, cilantro, or parsley) sprinkled on top. Tzatziki, a Greek cucumber and yogurt dip, makes the ideal complement, or leave it off for a colorful vegan entrée. Zest the lemon before juicing it for the eggplant—you'll add this zest to the tzatziki (you can also add any green scallion parts remaining from the eggplant recipe). For variation, try substituting Aleppo pepper for the crushed red pepper flakes.

Place the eggplant in the slow cooker. Heat the oil in a 10-inch, heavy sauté pan over medium-high heat. When hot, add the bell peppers, onions, scallions, garlic, salt, oregano, dill, cinnamon, pepper flakes, and black pepper. Sauté, stirring with a wooden spoon, until the onions soften, about 4 minutes. Whisk in the tomato paste and flour and cook until the flour disappears, no more than 1 minute. Add the tomatoes, lemon juice, and honey, and simmer for 3 minutes. Pour over the eggplant. Cover the slow cooker and cook on high until the eggplant is tender, 2½ to 3 hours. Remove the garlic and serve the eggplant over couscous, if desired, with the tzatziki.

Cucumber Tzatziki

2 large cucumbers, peeled

3 cups plain Greek or regular yogurt

½ cup sliced scallions, green parts only (2 to 4)

¼ cup finely chopped fresh mint leaves

1 tablespoon plus 1 teaspoon minced garlic

1 teaspoon coarse salt

Zest of 1 lemon

5 grinds black pepper

Thick Greek yogurt is best for this cooling garlicky sauce.

Use the large holes of a box grater to shred the cucumbers, then squeeze and drain any liquid (you should have 2 cups of shredded, drained cucumber). Place in a medium bowl and stir in the remaining ingredients. Serve cold with the eggplant.

Spicy veggie chili with summer squash and jalapeños

SERVES 4 TO 6

¼ cup vegetable oil, divided

1½ cups red bell peppers, diced (about 1)

1½ cups green bell peppers, diced (about 1)

½ cup scallions, white, light green, and some dark green parts, thinly sliced (about 4)

2 tablespoons minced garlic

2 teaspoons minced jalapeño (1 small)

2 teaspoons coarse salt, divided

5 grinds black pepper

1 teaspoon chili powder

4 cups yellow summer squash, diced (about 2)

One 15-ounce can pinto beans, rinsed and drained

One 15-ounce can black beans, rinsed and drained

¼ cup tomato paste

2 tablespoons minced chiles or liquid from a can of chipotle chiles en adobo

2 tablespoons all-purpose flour

One 28-ounce can fire-roasted diced tomatoes, with juice

1 cup low-sodium vegetable stock

3 tablespoons fresh-squeezed, strained lime juice

½ cup coarsely chopped fresh cilantro leaves

Tortilla chips, for serving (optional)

Diced avocado, for serving (optional)

Sour cream, for serving (optional)

This colorful chili is delicious with sour cream, diced avocados, and warm tortillas or lime-flavored tortilla chips. For less heat, omit the jalapeño.

1. Heat half of the oil in a 10-inch, heavy sauté pan over medium-high heat. When warm, add the bell peppers, scallions, garlic, jalapeño, half of the salt, the black pepper, and chili powder, and sauté until the vegetables are softened, about 6 minutes. Add the squash and sauté until slightly softened, another 3 minutes. Transfer to the slow cooker, add the beans, and mix well.

2. Reduce the heat to medium under the sauté pan and add the remaining oil, plus the tomato paste, chiles or chipotle liquid, and flour. Cook until the mixture is thickened and the flour disappears, about 1 minute. Increase the heat to high and add the tomatoes with their juices, the stock, lime juice, and remaining salt. Boil, stirring well, for 2 minutes, and pour into the slow cooker. Cover and cook on low to meld the flavors, 3 to 4 hours. Stir in the cilantro, and serve with the chips, avocado, and sour cream, if desired.

Indian chickpeas with golden raisins and cucumber raita

SERVES 6

1 pound dried chickpeas

2 tablespoons vegetable oil

1 red onion, halved and coarsely chopped

1⅓ cups finely chopped peeled carrots

6 large whole cloves garlic

2 scant tablespoons minced peeled ginger root

1 tablespoon garam masala

1 teaspoon minced jalapeño (seeds and membranes removed)

¼ cup tomato paste

¼ cup all-purpose flour

One 28-ounce can whole peeled tomatoes

2 cups low-sodium vegetable or chicken stock

½ cup golden raisins

¼ cup fresh-squeezed, strained lime juice

2 tablespoons dark brown sugar

2 teaspoons coarse salt

Cucumber Raita (recipe on the facing page)

This traditional North Indian dish known as *channa masala* is delicious served over basmati rice, with raita (Indian cucumber yogurt sauce) on the side. To keep the flavor true to the traditional version, choose a garam masala (Indian spice mixture) without salt and use unflavored peeled tomatoes. It's up to you whether you remove the whole garlic.

1. Pour the chickpeas into a large bowl, cover with several inches of water, and soak overnight. After soaking, pour into a colander set in the sink. Rinse with water, then drain. Pour the soaked, rinsed, and drained beans into the slow cooker.

2. Heat the oil in a 10-inch, heavy sauté pan over medium-high heat. When hot, add the onions, carrots, garlic, ginger, garam masala, and jalapeño, and sauté until the onions are softened, about 6 minutes. Whisk in the tomato paste and flour and cook until the flour disappears, no more than 1 minute. Add the tomatoes, stock, raisins, lime juice, and sugar and raise the heat to high. Cook, whisking and smashing the tomatoes a bit, for about another 6 minutes. Pour over the chickpeas in the slow cooker, cover, and cook on low until the chickpeas are tender, 8 to 10 hours. Remove the whole garlic, if desired, and season with the salt. Serve with Cucumber Raita on the side.

Cucumber Raita

One 32-ounce container low-fat plain yogurt

1¾ cups peeled, seeded, and finely chopped cucumbers (about 1 large)

¾ cup shredded peeled carrots (about 1 small)

½ cup finely chopped cilantro, parsley, or mint leaves

1 teaspoon coarse salt

1 teaspoon granulated sugar

¾ teaspoon ground cumin

¼ teaspoon ground ginger

5 grinds black pepper

The low-fat yogurt simulates the watery nature of authentic raita.

Mix together all of the ingredients in a medium bowl and chill. Leftovers will keep for up to 3 days.

Slow-cooked ratatouille over goat cheese polenta

SERVES 8

FOR THE RATATOUILLE

Cooking spray

2 large eggplants, peeled and cut into ½-inch pieces (about 10½ cups)

3 medium zucchini or yellow summer squash, cut into ½-inch pieces (about 6½ cups)

3 tablespoons coarse salt

3 tablespoons unsalted butter, divided

2 small to medium red onions, halved and thinly sliced (about 3½ cups)

2 red bell peppers, cut into ½-inch pieces (about 3 cups)

3 tablespoons finely chopped garlic

¼ cup all-purpose flour

¼ cup tomato paste

One 28-ounce can whole peeled tomatoes

1 tablespoon finely chopped fresh thyme leaves

10 grinds black pepper

½ cup packed freshly grated Parmigiano-Reggiano (about ¼ pound)

1 cup coarsely chopped fresh basil leaves

FOR THE POLENTA

6 cups low-sodium vegetable or chicken stock

1½ teaspoons coarse salt

1½ cups polenta or coarse-ground cornmeal (not instant)

½ stick unsalted butter

4 ounces fresh goat cheese (about ½ cup)

10 grinds black pepper

Parmigiano-Reggiano adds salty, nutty richness to this ratatouille, which rivals the best oven versions. To speed preparation, feel free to skip the first step of salting and rinsing the eggplant and zucchini (this process draws off any bitter juices). Instead, just remove any particularly seedy and brown parts of the eggplant, or use smaller Japanese eggplants (which also do not need to be peeled). For pizzazz, add chickpeas and pitted, chopped oil-cured black olives. To make this dish vegan, swap in olive oil for the butter and skip the cheese (adding olives will make up for cheese's saltiness).

When reheating the polenta, add liquid (such as chicken stock or milk), then adjust the seasoning if necessary with more salt, pepper, and butter.

MAKE THE RATATOUILLE

1. Grease the slow cooker with cooking spray.

2. Place the eggplant and zucchini in a large colander and toss well with 3 tablespoons of the salt; let sit for about 45 minutes. Rinse well to remove the salt, then dry well, gently squeezing out excess water with a kitchen towel. Add to the greased

continued

slow cooker. Heat 2 tablespoons of the butter in a 10-inch, heavy sauté pan over medium-high heat. When warm, add the onions, bell peppers, and garlic and sauté until the vegetables are softened, about 8 minutes. Transfer to the slow cooker. Reduce the heat to medium and add the remaining 1 tablespoon of butter. As soon as it melts, add the flour and tomato paste, and cook until the mixture is thickened and the flour disappears, about 1 minute. Increase the heat to medium high and add the tomatoes with their juices, thyme, and pepper. Cook, crushing the tomatoes a bit with a wooden spoon, until thickened and smooth, about 6 minutes. Mix with the vegetables in the slow cooker. Cover the slow cooker and cook on low until the vegetables are tender, 4 to 5 hours. Uncover and remove from the heat; immediately stir in the cheese and basil.

MAKE THE POLENTA
While the ratatouille is cooking, add the stock and salt to a medium, heavy saucepan and bring to a boil over medium-high heat. Once boiling, gradually whisk in the cornmeal. Reduce the heat to low, and cook, stirring every 3 minutes, until creamy and thickened, 30 to 35 minutes. Remove from the heat and stir in the butter, cheese, and pepper.

TO SERVE
Ladle polenta into individual bowls, spoon ratatouille on top, and serve immediately.

- **PREP TIME FOR PORK:** About 10 minutes   ▪ **PREP TIME FOR SAUCE:** 45 minutes to 1 hour
- **PREP TIME FOR PICKLES:** About 30 minutes active time and another few hours or overnight in the fridge   ▪ **SLOW COOKER TIME:** About 7½ hours

Pulled pork sandwiches with peach barbecue sauce and pickled cucumber and fennel

SERVES 6

FOR THE PORK

¼ cup plus 2 tablespoons yellow mustard

¼ cup light brown sugar

2 teaspoons coarse salt

1½ teaspoons chile powder

15 grinds black pepper

5 pounds bone-in pork shoulder, well trimmed of fat and skin

3 cups low-sodium chicken stock

FOR THE BARBECUE SAUCE

8 ripe peaches

1 tablespoon vegetable oil

2 cups finely chopped red onions (about 1 large)

1 tablespoon peeled minced ginger root

1 tablespoon minced garlic

½ teaspoon chile powder

One 28-ounce can tomato purée (without basil)

¼ cup blackstrap molasses

3 tablespoons honey

2 tablespoons cider vinegar

1 tablespoon yellow mustard

1 tablespoon fresh-squeezed, strained lemon juice

1 tablespoon liquid from a can of chipotle chiles en adobo

1½ teaspoons coarse salt

8 grinds black pepper

FOR THE PICKLES

1 large English cucumber, ends trimmed and remainder sliced ¼ inch thick

2½ cups fennel, core removed and thinly sliced (about ½ large bulb)

2 cups cider vinegar

½ cup plus 2 tablespoons granulated sugar

6 whole cloves garlic

1 teaspoon yellow mustard seeds

1 teaspoon whole coriander seeds

1 teaspoon whole black peppercorns

1 teaspoon coarse salt

2 dried bay leaves

½ teaspoon whole cloves

1 large bunch fresh dill

FOR SERVING

6 hamburger buns, halved and toasted

This standout dish features a homemade seasonal barbecue sauce and homemade quick pickles. The sauce recipe makes about double what you need (roughly 6 cups); you can safely halve it, if you like. Prepare the sauce while the pork cooks. Taste the sauce and adjust its sweetness, depending on the peaches you use.

continued

MAKE THE PORK

Mix together the mustard, brown sugar, salt, chile powder, and pepper in the slow cooker. Add the pork and rub it all over with this mixture. Pour the stock on top, cover, and cook on low until the meat is fall-off-the-bone tender, about 7½ hours.

MAKE THE SAUCE

1. Cut an "X" in the bottom of each peach. Fill a large bowl with ice water. Fill a large saucepan with water, cover, and bring to a boil over high heat. When the water is boiling, add the peaches and cook for 2 minutes. Transfer to the ice-water bath. After a minute or so, remove and peel each peach (the skin should easily fall away from the flesh), then cut into 1-inch dice (you should have about 5 cups of chopped fruit). Set aside.

2. Add the oil to a heavy, medium-size saucepan and heat over medium high. When hot, add the onions, ginger, garlic, and chile powder, and sauté until softened, about 4 minutes. Add the remaining sauce ingredients and bring to a boil over high heat. Once boiling, reduce to a simmer over medium-low heat until the peaches break down into the sauce, 15 to 25 minutes; mash with a potato masher. If you'd like a very smooth sauce, carefully purée in the blender (in batches) or food processor. Set aside.

MAKE THE PICKLES

Place the cucumber and fennel in a large shallow container. Add the remaining pickle ingredients to a heavy, medium saucepan, and bring to a boil over high heat. Once the mixture has come to a boil, pour it over the vegetables. Let sit until it reaches room temperature, then cover and transfer to the fridge. Ideally, let the mixture steep at least overnight or up to 2 days before serving.

FINISH THE DISH AND SERVE

1. Once the meat is cooked, carefully transfer it to a cutting board. Shred the meat and discard any bones and gelatinous cartilage. Place the shredded meat in a large bowl, stir in about 3 cups of the sauce, and mix. Drain the pickles.

2. Spoon some pulled pork onto the buns, spoon well-drained pickles alongside, and serve, with extra sauce in a bowl, if desired.

Cod with puttanesca sauce and fresh-tomato toast

SERVES 4 TO 6

¼ cup plus 2 tablespoons olive oil, divided

2 cups red onions, finely chopped (about 1)

3 tablespoons minced garlic, divided

One 2-ounce tin anchovies in oil and salt, drained and finely chopped (about 2 tablespoons)

¼ teaspoon crushed red pepper flakes

3 tablespoons all-purpose flour

¼ cup tomato paste

One 28-ounce can whole peeled tomatoes

1 scant cup fresh-squeezed, strained orange juice, divided

½ cup oil-cured black olives, pitted and coarsely chopped

¼ cup capers, rinsed and drained

24 grinds black pepper, divided

2 pounds cod fillets, cut into 4 to 6 pieces (individual serving sizes)

2 tablespoons fresh-squeezed, strained lemon juice, divided

7 sprigs fresh thyme

1 teaspoon coarse salt

½ cup finely chopped fresh flat-leaf parsley leaves, divided

Fresh Tomato Toast (recipe on p. 139)

My version of the traditional Spanish *pan de tomate*, or tomato bread—with ripe seasonal tomatoes and lots of pungent garlic—makes a delicious accompaniment to the stewlike cod puttanesca. For variation, you can serve the cod with spaghetti, couscous, polenta, or toasted Italian bread. You can also vary the fish, swapping in sea bass for the cod.

1. Heat 2 tablespoons of the oil in a 10-inch, heavy sauté pan over medium-high heat. When hot, add the onions, 2 tablespoons of the garlic, the anchovies, and red pepper flakes, and sauté until the onions are softened and a bit golden brown, about 4 minutes. Stir in the flour and tomato paste, and cook until the mixture is a bit thickened and no flour is visible, about 1 minute. Add the canned tomatoes with their juices and ¼ cup plus 2 tablespoons orange juice, and bring to a boil over medium-high heat, crushing the tomatoes with a wooden spoon. Boil until thickened and relatively smooth, about 2 minutes. Add the olives, capers, and 8 grinds of black pepper, and pour into the slow cooker. Cover and cook on low until aromatic, about 2 hours.　　　　　　　　　　　　　　　　*continued*

2. About 30 minutes before the sauce will be done, marinate the fish with the remaining ¼ cup olive oil, remaining ½ cup orange juice, the lemon juice, thyme, and remaining 1 tablespoon garlic. Remove the fish from the marinade, discard the marinade (including the thyme sprigs), and season evenly on both sides with the salt and remaining 16 grinds pepper. Place the cod pieces in the slow cooker, gently pushing them down into the sauce, re-cover, and heat on low until cooked (opaque and flaky when tested with a fork), about 45 minutes. Gently stir the sauce to blend any white juices released from the fish into the sauce and mix in the parsley. Ladle the fish and sauce into shallow bowls and serve with the Fresh Tomato Toast.

Fresh Tomato Toast

MAKES ABOUT 1½ CUPS

2 heaping tablespoons minced garlic

⅔ cup extra-virgin olive oil, divided

1 large baguette, thinly sliced on the bias (about fifteen ½-inch-thick slices)

2 large ripe tomatoes, halved horizontally (not through the stem or root end)

¾ teaspoon coarse salt

7 grinds black pepper

This simple accompaniment is also delicious alone—in fact, it's a common breakfast in Spain.

Heat the oven to 400°F. Place the garlic and oil in a small bowl and let sit for at least 15 minutes; pour into a small strainer set over another small bowl. Discard the garlic and reserve the oil. Place the bread slices on a baking sheet. Brush with all but about 2 tablespoons of the garlic oil, and toast the bread in the oven until crisp and aromatic, about 15 minutes. Meanwhile, using the large holes of a box grater placed in a large bowl, grate the pulp or flesh side of each tomato half (this will yield about 1⅓ cups pulp). Discard the tomato skins. Add remaining 2 tablespoons garlic oil and the salt and pepper to the pulp. Top each baguette slice with some of the tomato mixture, and serve with the fish.

Pulled chicken with cherry-chile barbecue sauce

SERVES 4 TO 6

2 tablespoons vegetable oil

½ cup coarsely chopped shallots (about 1 large)

1 tablespoon peeled chopped fresh ginger (about one 1½-inch piece)

1 teaspoon minced fresh jalapeño (seeds and membranes removed)

Scant 4 cups dark sweet fresh cherries, pitted and de-stemmed (3 cups afterwards)

Two 14½-ounce cans diced tomatoes, no salt added (you'll only use 1½ cans; save the rest for another use)

¼ cup blackstrap molasses

¼ cup cider vinegar

1 tablespoon chipotle chile from a can of chipotle chiles en adobo

3 tablespoons Dijon mustard, divided

1¼ teaspoons chile powder, divided

2 teaspoons coarse salt, divided

15 grinds black pepper, divided

2 teaspoons light brown sugar

3 pounds bone-in, skinless chicken thighs, trimmed if necessary (about 8)

4 to 6 warmed burger buns, for serving

This fresh seasonal sauce—so good you'll be glad to have leftovers—features less sugar than traditional barbecue sauces. Serve the moist, flavorful chicken on warmed burger buns.

Wear rubber gloves when mincing the jalapeño so you don't burn your hands. When prepping the fresh cherries, wear a dark shirt, use a good cherry pitter, and work over two bowls: one for the pits and stems and the other for the usable flesh. Feel into the center of each cherry after pitting and de-stemming to make sure that no pit remains.

1. Heat the oil in a large heavy saucepan over medium-high heat. When hot, add the shallots, ginger, and jalapeño and sauté until softened, about 2 minutes. Add the cherries, tomatoes, molasses, vinegar, chipotle, 1 tablespoon mustard, ¾ teaspoon chile powder, 1½ teaspoons salt, and 5 grinds pepper, and bring to a boil over high heat. Reduce to a simmer over medium heat, and cook until aromatic and thickened, about 5 minutes. Remove from the heat and carefully transfer half to a blender; purée until smooth, about 20 seconds. Purée the second half until smooth (you should have about 5¼ cups). Set aside.

continued

2. Meanwhile, mix 2 tablespoons mustard, ½ teaspoon chile powder, ½ teaspoons salt, 10 grinds pepper, and the brown sugar in a large bowl; add the chicken and mix well with your hands. Put the chicken in the bottom of the slow cooker and pour 1½ cups of the barbecue sauce on top (reserve the remainder for serving and extras). Cover and cook on low until the meat is cooked through and tender, 4 to 4½ hours.

3. Use tongs to transfer the chicken to a cutting board and carefully use a fork to separate the meat from the bones, discarding the bones (you should have about 4 cups meat).

4. To serve, stir together 1 cup of the remaining sauce and the shredded meat, and reheat in the microwave or on the stovetop. Spoon some meat and sauce onto the bottom half of each bun, cover with the top bun, and serve.

Summer pork stew with peppers, cornmeal dumplings, and tomatillo salsa

SERVES 4 TO 6

FOR THE STEW

⅓ cup all-purpose flour

1 teaspoon coarse salt

1 teaspoon cumin

1 teaspoon dried oregano

10 grinds black pepper

2 pounds trimmed pork butt or shoulder, cut into 1½- to-2-inch cubes

2 tablespoons vegetable oil

2½ cups red onions, coarsely chopped (about 1 large)

1 cup red bell peppers, coarsely chopped (about 1)

1 cup green bell peppers, coarsely chopped (about 1)

8 whole garlic cloves

2 tablespoons minced jalapeño, seeds and membranes removed

¼ cup tomato paste

One 28-ounce can whole peeled tomatoes (without basil)

⅓ cup fresh-squeezed, strained orange juice

¼ cup fresh-squeezed, strained lime juice

2 tablespoons honey

FOR THE DUMPLINGS

⅔ cup all-purpose flour

⅓ cup whole-grain corn flour (I like Bob's Red Mill® brand)

2 teaspoons light brown sugar

1 teaspoon baking powder

½ teaspoon coarse salt

1 tablespoon unsalted butter

½ cup 2% or whole milk

FOR SERVING

Tomatillo Salsa (recipe on p. 144)

Sour cream (optional)

Shredded Cheddar or Monterey Jack cheese (optional)

Diced avocado (optional)

This stew is full of Mexican flavor, thanks to cumin, jalapeños, and cornmeal. Add sour cream, avocado, and shredded Cheddar or Monterey Jack on top.

   Ask your butcher to trim the pork shoulder before printing out the price. Once, I ended up removing ½ pound of fat from a 2½-pound pork shoulder!

1. In a medium-large bowl, mix together the flour, salt, cumin, oregano, and black pepper. Add the meat and dredge in the flour, shaking off and reserving any excess flour. Meanwhile, heat the oil in a 10-inch, heavy sauté pan over medium-high heat. When the oil is hot, add half of the meat and cook until golden brown on both sides;

continued

transfer to the slow cooker, then cook the rest of the meat, about 17 minutes total for both batches. Transfer all of the meat to the slow cooker.

2. Add the onions, bell peppers, garlic, and jalapeño to the hot pan, and sauté until the onions are softened, about 5 minutes. Whisk in the reserved seasoned flour and the tomato paste, and cook until the flour disappears, no more than 1 minute. Add the tomatoes, orange and lime juices, and honey, and raise the heat to high. Simmer for 2 minutes, and then pour over the pork. Cover and cook on low until the meat is cooked through and the meat and vegetables are tender, about 6 hours.

3. About 15 minutes before that time has elapsed, whisk together all of the dumpling dry ingredients in a medium bowl. With your hands, gently mix in the butter, then the milk (the dough will be sticky). Shape into six balls. Uncover the slow cooker and place the dumplings evenly on top of the stew. Re-cover and cook on high until the dumplings are cooked through, about 1 hour. Serve with Tomatillo Salsa and, if desired, sour cream, cheese, and avocado.

Tomatillo Salsa

MAKES ABOUT 1½ CUPS

2 cups finely chopped de-husked tomatillos	¼ cup finely chopped fresh cilantro leaves	2 teaspoons minced garlic
1 cup finely chopped red onions (about ½ large)	¼ cup fresh-squeezed, strained lime juice	¼ teaspoon coarse salt
		5 grinds black pepper

With just a few ingredients, this tart green salsa is intensely flavored and simple to prepare.

Combine all of the ingredients in a medium bowl and serve with the stew.

■ **PREP TIME:** About 30 minutes　　■ **SLOW COOKER TIME:** About 9 hours

Braised Greek beans with bell peppers and Greek yogurt

SERVES 6 AS AN ENTRÉE, MORE AS AN APPETIZER

FOR THE BEANS

1 pound dried large lima beans, covered by a few inches of water, soaked overnight, and drained (water discarded)

2 tablespoons olive oil

1¼ cups finely chopped green bell peppers (about 1 large, seeds and membranes removed)

1¼ cups finely chopped onions (about 1 small)

1 cup finely chopped peeled carrots (about 1 large)

½ cup finely chopped celery (about 1 large stalk)

2 tablespoons minced garlic (about 8 large cloves)

One 28-ounce can tomato purée (without basil)

2 cups low-sodium vegetable or chicken stock

¼ cup tomato paste

2 tablespoons honey

1 teaspoon dried dill

1 teaspoon dried oregano

6 grinds black pepper

2 tablespoons finely chopped fresh dill fronds

2 teaspoons coarse salt

FOR THE DILLED YOGURT

2 cups plain Greek yogurt

½ cup minced fresh dill fronds

1 tablespoon honey

½ teaspoon coarse salt

5 grinds black pepper

Inspired by *gigantes*, a traditional Greek dish, this healthy vegetarian starter or entrée stars giant lima beans. Without the yogurt, it's vegan (but the dilled Greek yogurt is absolutely delicious!). Make sure to soak the beans overnight, then begin the dish in the morning. Add the salt after the beans have cooked to avoid making them tough.

1. Pour the drained beans into the slow cooker. Heat the oil in a heavy, medium-size saucepan over medium-high heat. When hot, add the bell peppers, onions, carrots, celery, and garlic, and sauté until softened, about 5 minutes. Whisk in the tomato purée, stock, tomato paste, honey, dill, oregano, and black pepper, and raise the heat to high. Simmer, whisking, for about 5 minutes. Pour over the beans, making sure they're all submerged in the liquid. Cover and cook on low until the beans are tender, about 9 hours. Season with the fresh dill and salt.

2. While the beans are cooking, stir together the yogurt ingredients.

3. Serve the beans in individual portions, each topped with a dollop of yogurt.

BUILDING ATTRACTIVE MEALS

Let's be honest: Gorgeous food isn't exactly the slow cooker's forte. After all, the end result of slow cooking is delicious, fork-tender stews, which means colors won't always be vivid and ingredients won't always look distinct. Likewise, don't expect golden-on-the-outside and rosy-on-the-inside, crisp-edged slices of beef. Instead, you'll have meat that breaks apart rather than slices cleanly.

When working with big cuts of beef, pork, or veal, first let the meat rest for about 15 minutes after cooking. Then use a sharp serrated knife and cut thinly against the grain, in the opposite direction of the fibers (shown at right).

Other than setting your expectations realistically, you can use a few tactics to make slow-cooker dishes look more attractive. With many tender green vegetables, such as asparagus, cook them quickly on the stove to preserve their hue. With beets—which could stain an entire dish red—roast them in the oven and stir them in at the last minute. If you won't be eating a dish immediately, wait until right before serving to add delicate ingredients, such as peas, herbs, greens, or chopped fresh tangerines.

In general, to achieve food that pops with excitement, shoot for dishes with a balance of color, texture, and flavor. Aim for at least three hues, at minimum one crispy or crunchy element, and a balance of salty, sweet, sour, and savory flavors. Fresh ingredients, such as herbs, add sparks of color. Croutons, toast, tortilla chips, or fried plantains supply crunch. Citrus juice, fresh herbs, and other garnishes boost flavor.

For a refined presentation, remove cheesecloth flavor sachets, whole garlic, and bones (or tie flesh to bones with kitchen twine after browning meat and remember to remove the twine before serving). Shallow plain white bowls will, in most cases, display stews beautifully. Pour loose puddings, such as rice puddings, into large bowls for serving family style or into individual parfait glasses.

Bell peppers stuffed with Latin beef picadillo

SERVES 6

½ cup raisins

¼ cup rum (not spiced or coconut flavored)

One 28-ounce can tomato purée (without basil)

½ cup low-sodium vegetable or chicken stock

¼ cup cider vinegar, divided

2 teaspoons coarse salt, divided

20 grinds black pepper, divided

1¾ teaspoons ground cumin, divided

6 large red bell peppers

2 slices white sandwich bread

½ cup 2% or whole milk

Scant 2 pounds ground beef chuck

2 tablespoons olive oil

2 cups finely chopped red onions (about 1)

1½ cups finely chopped green bell peppers, seeds and membranes discarded (about 1)

2 tablespoons minced garlic

1 teaspoon ground allspice

½ teaspoon dried oregano

¼ teaspoon ground coriander

⅛ teaspoon ground cayenne

½ cup plus 2 tablespoons tomato paste

¾ cup pitted pimento-stuffed Spanish (green) olives, finely chopped

1 tablespoon plus 1 teaspoon capers, rinsed and drained

2 teaspoons light brown sugar

Featuring a twist on the classic Cuban picadillo (sweet meat stuffing), this yummy, sweet-and-sour dish is gorgeous served family style on a platter over white rice, with fried plantains on the side. Although this recipe contains a lot of ingredients, it's easy to prepare and worth the time—and the cook gets to eat any leftover stuffing for lunch!

To make this dish vegetarian, swap canned beans for the meat-bread mixture.

1. Combine the raisins and rum in a small bowl. Let sit for about an hour, then pour into a small strainer set over a small bowl. Keep the raisins and discard the rum. Pour the tomato purée, stock, 2 tablespoons of the vinegar, 1 teaspoon of the salt, 10 grinds of the pepper, and ¼ teaspoon of the cumin into the slow cooker. Mix well.

2. To cut the red bell peppers, use a paring knife to carefully cut off the top, slicing around the top about ½ inch down from the stem; set the top aside. Remove the membranes and seeds by cutting carefully around the inside of the pepper; discard the membranes and seeds. Stand the red peppers, without tops, on top of the sauce in the slow cooker. They should fit snugly. *continued*

3. In a large bowl, combine the bread and milk, and mash together with your hands or a fork until relatively smooth. Add the beef and gently knead to combine well (but don't overmix).

4. Heat the oil in a 10-inch, heavy sauté pan over medium-high heat. When hot, add the onions, green peppers, garlic, remaining 1½ teaspoons cumin, the allspice, oregano, coriander, and cayenne, and sauté until the vegetables have softened, about 5 minutes. Add the meat-bread mix, pressing down on it with a wooden spoon, the remaining 1 teaspoon salt, and remaining 10 grinds pepper. Sauté until the meat no longer looks raw, about 7 minutes. Stir in the drained raisins, remaining 2 tablespoons vinegar, the tomato paste, olives, capers, and brown sugar, and simmer for 7 minutes. Spoon the mixture into the bell peppers, pressing down to fit as much as possible within their cavities—it will spill over. Then cover the peppers with their reserved tops.

5. Cover the slow cooker and cook on low until the peppers are tender, about 5 hours. Very carefully transfer to a plate or platter, keeping the tops on. Serve, spooning some cooking liquid from the slow cooker alongside if you like.

Triple-apricot "French toast" bread pudding with sea salt caramel sauce

SERVES 8

FOR THE BREAD PUDDING

Cooking spray

1 large loaf challah or brioche (about 15 ounces), cut into 1-inch cubes (about 12 cups)

2 cups thick apricot nectar, such as Looza

2 cups dried apricots

2½ cups heavy cream

2½ cups whole milk

1½ cups granulated sugar

9 large egg yolks

1 tablespoon plus 1 teaspoon vanilla bean paste or pure vanilla extract

Scant tablespoon freshly grated lemon zest (about 1 lemon)

¾ teaspoon coarse salt

½ teaspoon ground cinnamon, divided

2 tablespoons light brown sugar

FOR THE SEA SALT CARAMEL SAUCE

1½ cups heavy cream

1 cup dark brown sugar

½ stick unsalted butter

¼ teaspoon sea salt

1 teaspoon vanilla bean paste or pure vanilla extract

FOR THE SAUTÉED STONE FRUIT TOPPING

2 tablespoons unsalted butter

2 large slightly ripe peaches, pitted and thinly sliced

4 slightly ripe apricots, pitted and thinly sliced

2 to 3 tablespoons honey, to taste

1 tablespoon fresh-squeezed, strained lemon juice

¼ teaspoon coarse salt

This rich dessert pairs three apricot ingredients with the most delicious salted caramel sauce. Purchase sulfured dried apricots, which are a pretty color, and look for a thick, intensely flavored apricot juice drink (I love Looza brand). Although you might be tempted to toss some fresh apricots into the bread pudding, resist. Using fresh fruit would make the pudding watery.

Be sure to line the slow cooker insert with heavy-duty aluminum foil to prevent burning (for more on this, see p. 211).

MAKE THE BREAD PUDDING

Heat the oven to 300°F. Line your slow cooker to cover the hot spot and make it easy to remove the finished bread pudding (see the sidebar on p. 211 for how to do this).

continued

Spray the foil with cooking spray. Place the bread on a baking sheet and toast in the oven until dry, about 30 minutes. Add to the slow cooker. Put the apricot nectar in a medium bowl and microwave until hot, about 1 minute. Add the dried apricots and let sit for 20 minutes; drain and discard (or drink!) the nectar, and dice the apricots (you should have about 2¼ cups). Add to the slow cooker, mixing gently with the bread. In a large bowl, whisk together the cream, milk, sugar, yolks, vanilla, lemon zest, salt, and ¼ teaspoon cinnamon. Pour over the bread mix and press down with a wooden spoon until well moistened. In a small bowl, mix the remaining ¼ teaspoon cinnamon and brown sugar and sprinkle on top. Cover and cook on low until firm in the center, about 4 hours. Let sit for 30 minutes before serving.

MAKE THE CARAMEL SAUCE
Add the first three sauce ingredients to a heavy, deep, medium-size saucepan. Bring to a boil over medium-high heat, stirring frequently. Lower the heat to medium low, stir in the salt, and simmer, stirring occasionally, until the sauce becomes a brownish orange color and coats the back of a spoon, about 10 minutes (you should have 1½ to 2 cups). Remove the pan from the heat and stir in the vanilla.

MAKE THE FRUIT TOPPING
Add the butter to a 10-inch, heavy sauté pan and heat over medium until melted. Add the remaining topping ingredients, mix gently with a wooden spoon, and cook until softened, about 5 minutes (you should have about 6 cups of fruit).

TO SERVE
Add a slice of bread pudding to each dessert dish. Spoon some of the fruit topping alongside it, and drizzle both with the caramel sauce. Serve.

Corn-vanilla pudding with triple-berry sauce

SERVES 6

FOR THE PUDDING

1 tablespoon unsalted butter, softened

One 14-ounce can sweetened condensed milk

1 cup fresh corn kernels (about 1 ear corn), or 1 cup frozen corn, thawed and drained

1 cup whole milk

4 large eggs, beaten

1 scant tablespoon freshly grated lemon zest (about 1 lemon)

2 teaspoons vanilla bean paste or pure vanilla extract

Pinch of coarse salt

FOR THE TRIPLE-BERRY SAUCE

1 quart mix of fresh blueberries, strawberries, and raspberries

½ cup granulated sugar

2 tablespoons fresh-squeezed, strained lemon juice

Pinch of salt

This unusual, aromatic dessert tastes like flan or vanilla crème brûlée. Studded with corn kernels and vanilla bean seeds, it resembles an elegant terrine—but is deceptively inexpensive to prepare. Make sure to remove any strings from the corn and scrape all of the condensed milk out of the can. For best results, use a loaf pan or small baking dish, and check to be sure that it fits inside your slow cooker.

1. Place a metal trivet (or a few sticks made of rolled-up foil) in the slow cooker. Grease the inside of a roughly 8- x 4-inch loaf pan with the butter. Add the condensed milk, corn, whole milk, eggs, lemon zest, vanilla, and salt to a large bowl and stir well. Pour into the loaf pan, cover tightly with foil, and place on the trivet or foil sticks. Pour about 2 cups of boiling water into the slow cooker around the pan. Cover and cook on high until the pudding is set on the sides but still jiggles a bit in the center, about 2 hours. Carefully remove the pan from the slow cooker and let cool to room temperature, about 20 minutes, then chill in the fridge for at least 1 hour.

2. Meanwhile, in a blender, purée the sauce ingredients until smooth, about 10 seconds. Pour into a large strainer set over a medium-size bowl. Use a spoon to press, scrape, and stir the berry mixture in the strainer, coaxing the finer, velvety sauce through its bottom into the bowl. Discard the solids in the strainer; you'll have about 2¾ cups sauce.

3. Serve slices or large dollops of the corn pudding, with the berry purée spooned over the top.

■ **PREP TIME:** About 40 minutes ■ **SLOW COOKER TIME:** About 2 hours
■ **COULIS TIME:** About 15 minutes

Cardamom-rosewater rice pudding with raspberry-rose coulis and toasted pistachios

SERVES 6 TO 8

Cooking spray

10 whole cardamom pods

3 cups 2% milk

3½ cups unflavored or plain soy creamer, such as Silk Creamer Original (not unsweetened)

1½ cups granulated sugar

3 tablespoons rosewater

½ teaspoon coarse salt

1½ cups medium-grain white rice, such as Arborio, rinsed with cold water and drained

½ cup golden raisins

Raspberry-Rose Coulis (recipe on the facing page)

½ cup shelled unsalted pistachios, lighted toasted and finely chopped

In this beguiling, simple-to-prepare dessert inspired by Indian cooking, the faintly tart raspberry sauce balances out the sweet, milky pudding. Delicious cold or warm, it can also be poured into a large bowl and served family style. As it chills, the pudding will thicken. Rosewater and cardamom pods can be found at Middle Eastern markets and natural- and gourmet-food stores. You can substitute ground cardamom for the cardamom pods and orange-flower water for the rose water, if you like.

To toast pistachios, spread them on a baking sheet and bake in a heated 350°F oven for about 10 minutes, until aromatic and just starting to become a very faint golden brown. Then, while warm, rub in a clean kitchen towel to remove the skins.

1. Grease the slow cooker with cooking spray. Place the cardamom pods on a small piece of cheesecloth and use the side of the blade of a chef's knife to crush them. Form into a bundle and secure tightly with kitchen twine. Add to a medium-size, heavy saucepan, along with the milk, soy creamer, sugar, rosewater, and salt. Stir and bring to a strong simmer over medium-high heat, which could take up to 20 minutes (watch carefully so the milk mixture doesn't boil).

2. Pour the hot mixture, including the cardamom sachet, into the slow cooker. Add the rice and raisins, and stir well. Cover and cook on low until the rice is completely tender, about 2 hours (you want there to be some liquid left). Remove from the heat and discard the sachet.

3. Let the rice mixture cool slightly, then pour into individual serving bowls; cover and refrigerate until cold, about 2 hours. Drizzle each serving with Raspberry-Rose Coulis, sprinkle with pistachios, and serve.

Rasberry-Rose Coulis

**MAKES A
GENEROUS 1¼ CUPS**

2 cups (about 10 to 11 ounces) fresh raspberries	1 tablespoon fresh-squeezed, strained lemon juice
¼ cup granulated or superfine sugar	1 tablespoon rosewater
	⅛ teaspoon coarse salt

Rosewater makes this fresh sauce incredibly aromatic and just a touch exotic.

Purée the sauce ingredients in a blender until smooth, about 10 seconds. Pour into a large strainer set over a medium-size bowl. Use a spoon to press, scrape, and stir the berry mixture in the strainer, coaxing the finer, velvety sauce through its bottom and into the bowl. Discard the solids in the strainer.

Fig preserves with brandy and vanilla bean

MAKES ABOUT 5 CUPS

2 large, juicy lemons, preferably organic

2 pounds brown turkey or other large figs (about 20), each de-stemmed and cut into 8 pieces

3½ cups granulated sugar

Pinch of coarse salt

2 tablespoons brandy

1 teaspoon vanilla bean paste or pure vanilla extract

5 tablespoons pectin powder, such as Ball Classic Pectin (not low sugar)

Dotted with fig seeds, these preserves are beautiful and sophisticated. Serve them with blue cheese, pound cake, vanilla ice cream, or Greek yogurt, or slather on dessert pizza. I left the skin on the figs, since it was think, smooth, and attractive. A jar of these fig preserves makes a wonderful hostess or holiday gift.

1. Place a small plate in the freezer. With a vegetable peeler, gently peel the yellow zest from one of the lemons. Place on a small piece of cheesecloth, bundle up, and tie into a bag with kitchen twine. Add to the slow cooker. Squeeze ¼ cup juice from both lemons into a strainer set over a small bowl (you'll use about 1½ lemons); discard the solids. Add the juice to the slow cooker. Put the figs into a bowl and crush with a potato masher (you should have 4 heaping cups when packed tightly). Pour into the slow cooker, along with the sugar and salt. Stir well. Cover and cook the mixture on low for about 3 hours, until the fruit is soft.

2. Transfer the fig mixture into a large saucepan, remove and discard the cheesecloth bag, and stir in the brandy and vanilla. Bring to a boil over medium-high heat. Add the pectin and boil for about 9 minutes, stirring occasionally and crushing the fruit with a potato masher, until the pectin has dissolved and the preserves have thickened. Remove the pot from the heat. To test whether the preserves have set, spoon a drop onto the chilled plate and tilt the plate. If the preserves run just a bit, they're done (if not, boil for another minute, then retest, but don't boil for much longer, or the pectin can break down).

3. Using a funnel, transfer the preserves into clean glass jars. Let them stand until cool, then cover and refrigerate. The preserves will last for 2 to 3 weeks in the refrigerator. If you'd like them to last longer, use the traditional canning method.

FALL

- Celeriac
- Chestnuts
- Kale
- Kohlrabi
- Parsley root

- Persimmons
- Quince
- Rutabagas
- Swiss chard
- Turnips

Hungarian beef goulash with yams and caramelized onions

SERVES 6

⅓ cup all-purpose flour

16 grinds black pepper, divided

1¼ teaspoons coarse salt, divided

1½ teaspoons ground paprika, divided

1½ teaspoons dried dill, divided

2 pounds beef chuck stew meat, cut into 1½- to 2-inch pieces

5 cups 1½- to 2-inch pieces peeled yams (about 2)

2 tablespoons unsalted butter

1¾ cups finely chopped red onions (about 1 large)

½ teaspoon granulated sugar

¼ cup vegetable oil, divided

5 cloves garlic

3 tablespoons tomato paste

1 tablespoon Dijon mustard

One 14-ounce can whole peeled tomatoes, with juice

¾ cup low-sodium chicken stock

⅓ cup thick apricot nectar, such as Looza

Minced fresh chives and dill, for garnish (optional)

Sweet potatoes add flavor and color to this Hungarian classic. Serve over egg noodles tossed with butter and fresh dill. I've left out the traditional sour cream, but if you want to include it, feel free to stir it in after the meat has cooked, but while it's still warm.

1. In a large bowl, mix together the flour with 10 grinds pepper, ½ teaspoon salt, and 1 teaspoon each paprika and dried dill. Add the meat and coat, shaking off and reserving any excess flour.

2. In the slow cooker, toss the yams with ½ teaspoon each salt, paprika, and dried dill, and 6 grinds pepper.

3. Heat the butter in a 10-inch, heavy sauté pan over medium heat. Once melted, add the onions plus ¼ teaspoon salt and the sugar, and let cook until golden brown, stirring only occasionally, about 16 minutes. Pour the caramelized onions over the yams, spooning all of them out of the pan.

4. While the pan is still hot, add half of the oil and raise the heat to medium high. Add half of the floured meat and cook until golden brown on both sides, about 6 minutes. Transfer it to the slow cooker. Repeat with the remaining meat and oil, about another 4 minutes. Transfer it to the slow cooker.

5. Add the garlic to the hot pan and cook for 1 minute. Add the reserved flour plus the tomato paste and mustard, and whisk until the flour disappears, about 1 minute. Add the tomatoes, stock, and nectar, and raise the heat to high. Cook, whisking, for 3 minutes, then pour over the meat.

6. Cover the slow cooker and cook on low until the meat and yams are tender, 7 to 8 hours. Let sit for about 5 minutes, then use a large spoon or ladle to skim fat off the surface. If desired, garnish with the fresh herbs, and serve.

SLOW COOKER SECRET

BUDGET-MINDED OPTIONS FOR THE SLOW COOKER

Using a slow cooker is inherently economical since you use cheap cuts of meat, dried beans, and other humble ingredients. Still, you can make these recipes even more budget-friendly. My number one tip: Substitute water for stock. Two, when meat needs to be trimmed, have the butcher do it for you before he or she weighs and prices out your order. Three, buy meat in bulk, such as family packs of beef chuck meat; freeze what you don't need for the recipe and simply defrost the rest when you need it. Finally, swap in dried herbs for fresh (though you won't get the same flavor punch in your recipe).

Beef bourguignon with mushrooms, turnips, rutabagas, and carrots

SERVES 6

12 ounces center-cut, uncured smoked bacon, chopped

½ cup all-purpose flour

2¾ teaspoons coarse salt, divided, plus more for cooking the onions

15 grinds black pepper

1 teaspoon dried thyme

1 teaspoon ground coriander

2¼ pounds beef chuck, cut into 1½- to 2-inch cubes

¼ cup plus 1 tablespoon vegetable oil, divided

1½ cups finely chopped peeled carrots (about 3 medium)

1½ cups finely chopped turnips (about 2 small)

1½ cups finely chopped white onions (about ¾ large)

1 cup finely chopped rutabaga (about 1 small)

9 whole cloves garlic

¼ cup tomato paste

¼ cup Dijon mustard

1 cup red wine

1 cup low-sodium chicken stock

3 tablespoons mild honey

2 dried bay leaves

2 tablespoons unsalted butter

10 ounces white button mushroom caps, quartered

6 ounces pearl onions, peeled

¼ cup finely chopped fresh flat-leaf parsley, for garnish

¼ cup finely minced fresh chives, for garnish

This sweet, smoky stew is complex and delicious. Using a bag of peeled pearl onions will save you a lot of time.

1. Place the bacon in a cold, 10-inch, heavy sauté pan, and heat over medium. Cook until most of the fat renders, about 10 minutes. Raise the heat to medium high and cook until slightly golden brown, another 3 to 4 minutes. Transfer to a paper-towel-lined plate, then to the slow cooker.

2. Meanwhile, in a large bowl, combine the flour with 2 teaspoons of the salt, the pepper, thyme, and coriander. Add the beef and coat, shaking off and reserving any excess flour. Add half of the meat to the pan of hot bacon fat and brown on all sides, about 7 minutes; transfer to the slow cooker. Repeat with the remaining meat, about another 7 minutes. (During this process, add oil if the pan dries out; you'll probably use about 3 tablespoons.)

3. Add another 2 tablespoons of oil to the pan, then add the carrots, turnips, onions, rutabagas, and garlic. Sauté until the onions begin to soften, about 5 minutes. Stir in the tomato paste, mustard, and the reserved flour, and cook until the flour is no longer visible, about 1 minute. Remove the pan from the heat and add the wine, then return the pan to the heat and raise the heat to high. Cook for 3 minutes, scraping the bottom of the pan with a wooden spoon. Add the stock, honey, and bay leaves, and cook for another 3 minutes. Pour this sauce over the bacon and beef in the slow cooker, cover, and cook on low until the meat is tender, 6 to 8 hours. Let sit for 5 minutes, then use a large spoon or ladle to skim the fat off the surface (there will be a good amount).

4. About 10 minutes before the stew is done cooking, heat the butter in a 10-inch, heavy sauté pan over medium high. When the butter has melted, add the mushrooms plus the remaining ¾ teaspoon salt and sauté until the mushrooms are cooked through and most of the liquid has evaporated, about 8 minutes. Drain and stir into the finished stew.

5. At the same time, fill a medium-size, heavy saucepan two-thirds full of heavily salted water and bring to a boil over high heat. Once boiling, add the pearl onions and cook until tender, about 4 minutes. Drain and stir into the finished stew.

6. Serve, garnishing each portion with fresh herbs.

SPOTLIGHT ON

TURNIPS

Roughly the size of beets, turnips are white and purple root vegetables. Once peeled, they can be cooked in myriad ways. Go with small, heavy turnips, which have a sweeter flavor than larger, woodier specimens. The roots should be firm and the leaves, if still attached, a vibrant green. Store turnips in the fridge for a couple of weeks or in a cool, dry place for longer.

Indian-style cauliflower, potato, and parsley root curry

SERVES 6

2 tablespoons unsalted butter or vegetable oil

2 cups finely chopped red onions (about 1 large)

2 tablespoons minced garlic

2 tablespoons minced fresh ginger

1 teaspoon minced fresh jalapeño

4 cups 1-inch cubes peeled Idaho or russet potatoes (about 4 to 5)

2 cups 1-inch cubes peeled parsley root (about 2 large)

1 teaspoon cumin

1 teaspoon curry powder

1 teaspoon ground coriander

1 teaspoon coarse salt

½ teaspoon ground turmeric

10 grinds black pepper

3 tablespoons tomato paste

2 tablespoons all-purpose flour

One 13½-ounce can light coconut milk, well shaken

One 14-ounce can whole peeled tomatoes, with juice

¼ cup fresh-squeezed, strained lime juice

2 tablespoons mild honey

3 cups 1-inch cauliflower florets (about 1 head cauliflower)

This vegetarian Indian-inspired dish is delicious served over rice accented with butter, peas, and fresh cilantro. Spoon some raita (Indian cucumber yogurt sauce) alongside; see the recipe on p. 131. Celeriac can take the place of parsley root.

1. Heat the butter or oil in a 10-inch, heavy frying pan over medium-high heat. When melted, add the onions, garlic, ginger, and jalapeño, and sauté until the onions are softened, about 3 minutes. Stir in the potatoes, parsley root, cumin, curry powder, coriander, salt, turmeric, and pepper, and sauté until the vegetables are coated, about 4 minutes. Pour into the slow cooker.

2. While the pan is hot, whisk in the tomato paste and flour and cook until no white flour is visible, no more than 1 minute. Add the coconut milk, tomatoes with their juice, lime juice, and honey, and whisk until thickened, about 4 minutes. Pour over the vegetables.

3. Cover and cook on low until tender, about 3 hours. Stir in the cauliflower, cover, raise the heat to high, and cook until all of the vegetables are tender, about another 1½ hours.

PARSLEY ROOT

Parsley root, a subspecies of parsley, is a mild beige root vegetable that tastes like a cross between carrots and celery. To prepare it, peel, dice, and roast or stew it. Look for firm roots with vibrantly colored leaves, and remove the leaves right before preparing the roots. Parsley root can keep in the fridge for up to a week. If you can't find it, substitute celeriac (or celery root).

Short ribs with stout, root vegetables, and sauerkraut

SERVES 4

½ cup all-purpose flour

3⅔ pounds bone-in beef chuck short ribs (about 5 pieces, each halved through the bone by your butcher)

2 teaspoons coarse salt, divided

20 grinds black pepper

2 tablespoons unsalted butter, divided

2 tablespoons vegetable oil, divided

1¾ cups finely chopped red onions (about 1 large)

1 cup finely chopped peeled parsnips (about 2)

¾ cup finely chopped peeled carrots (about 4 small)

8 whole cloves garlic

⅓ cup Dijon mustard

¼ cup tomato paste

1 cup stout beer, such as Guinness®

1 cup low-sodium chicken stock

⅔ cup drained sauerkraut

¼ cup honey

Serve this Irish-inspired, slightly sweet version of short ribs over potato purée or polenta. Stout beer, sauerkraut, and mustard add intense flavors.

1. Place the flour in a large bowl. Coat each short rib with the flour and place on a cutting board, reserving any remaining flour. Sprinkle all of the short ribs with a total of 1 teaspoon salt and all of the pepper.

2. Add half of the butter and half of the oil to a 10-inch, heavy sauté pan, and set over medium-high heat. When hot, add four of the short rib pieces and cook until golden brown on each side, about 5 minutes on the first side and 3 minutes on the second. Transfer to the bottom of the slow cooker in one layer. Repeat with two more batches of short ribs, using the remaining butter and oil in the process, a total of 15 to 20 minutes. (You might need to carefully clean out the pan with a paper towel if the bits get too brown.)

3. Pour off all but about 2 tablespoons fat from the pan. Add the onions, parsnips, carrots, and garlic, and sauté until the vegetables are softened, about 3 minutes. Add the mustard, tomato paste, and reserved flour, and whisk until the white flour is no longer visible, about 1 minute. Remove the pan from the heat and add the stout;

continued

return the pan to the heat and raise the heat to high. Cook, stirring, until thickened, about 1 minute. Add the stock, sauerkraut, honey, and remaining 1 teaspoon salt, and bring to a boil, whisking, about another 5 minutes. Pour over the short ribs.

4. Cover and cook on low until very tender, about 8 hours. Using a large spoon or ladle, skim the fat off the surface, remove the bones—if desired—and serve, spooning sauce atop each portion.

SLOW COOKER SECRET

TIME-SAVING TIPS

While meat browns or vegetables sauté, prep the other ingredients. If you don't have time to peel and chop fresh produce, buy precut produce available at most supermarkets (this is likely not as fresh as unpackaged vegetables, though). In a pinch, go with frozen (but thaw and drain before using), and do so without shame. Some frozen vegetables—like peas—are often sweeter than fresh! If you can't find a particular fruit or vegetable, such as kohlrabi, substitute something more common but similar in flavor and texture. Finally, if you don't have time to roast or peel garlic, purchase preroasted garlic and whole, peeled cloves of garlic (but avoid jarred preminced garlic, which is low in flavor).

Lentils with beets, carrots, mushrooms, and parsnips

SERVES 8

20 whole coriander seeds

2 dried bay leaves

6 whole black peppercorns

5 whole cloves

½ bunch fresh thyme

½ bunch fresh rosemary

½ pound uncured thick-cut bacon, cut into ½-inch pieces

l pound dried green lentils, rinsed and picked over (about 2 cups)

6 carrots, peeled, 2 left whole and 4 cut into ½-inch slices, divided

2 cups finely chopped yellow onions (about 1½)

2 cups finely chopped fennel (about 1 trimmed and cored bulb)

10 cloves garlic

¼ cup tomato paste

2 tablespoons all-purpose flour

3 tablespoons Dijon mustard

1 cup white wine, such as Sauvignon Blanc

7 cups low-sodium vegetable or chicken stock

2 tablespoons honey

1 cup ½-inch-diced peeled beets (about ¼ large)

1 cup ½-inch slices peeled parsnips (about 3)

¼ cup olive oil, divided

¾ teaspoon coarse salt, divided

½ teaspoon ground coriander, divided

8 grinds black pepper, divided

2½ cups ½-inch-diced portabella mushroom caps (about 2)

2 tablespoons white-wine or Champagne vinegar

½ cup finely chopped fresh flat-leaf parsley leaves

Colorful and nourishing, this dish features a long ingredient list, but it's simple to prepare. If you don't eat pork, omit the meat and increase the salt slightly or use vegetarian bacon or sausage. For convenience, you can make the roasted vegetables in advance. Roasting them as opposed to cooking them in the slow cooker delivers caramelized flavors.

1. Place the first six ingredients on a large piece of cheesecloth, form into a bundle, and secure with kitchen twine. Place the bacon in a single layer in a cold, large, heavy saucepan and heat over medium. Cook until most of the fat renders, about 8 minutes. Raise the heat to medium high and cook until golden brown and a

continued

bit crisp, stirring, about 6 minutes; transfer the bacon to the slow cooker (don't leave any bacon bits in the pan). Discard all but 2 tablespoons of the bacon fat. Quickly pour the dried lentils on top of the bacon in the slow cooker, nestle in the cheesecloth bag of spices, and add the whole carrots.

2. Add the onions, fennel, and garlic to the saucepan, and cook, stirring, until the onions are softened, about 5 minutes. Add the tomato paste, flour, and mustard. Cook, stirring, until no flour is visible, about 1 minute. Remove the pan from the heat and carefully add the wine; return the pan to the heat and bring to a boil over high heat. Boil, whisking, until the sauce is a bit thick, 2 to 3 minutes. Pour in the stock and honey, whisk well, and bring to a boil, 15 to 20 minutes. Pour over the bacon-lentil mixture in the slow cooker. Cover and cook on low until the lentils are tender, 5½ to 6 hours.

3. Meanwhile, heat the oven to 400°F. When hot, place the beets, carrots, and parsnips on a rimmed baking sheet and toss with 2 tablespoons of the oil, ½ teaspoon salt, ¼ teaspoon coriander, and 4 grinds pepper. On another rimmed baking sheet, toss the mushrooms with the remaining 2 tablespoons of the oil, ¼ teaspoon salt, 4 grinds pepper, and ⅛ teaspoon coriander. Roast until the vegetables are tender, about 20 minutes for the mushrooms and 30 minutes for the root vegetables.

4. Remove the whole carrots, spice bag, and garlic from the lentils. Stir in the cooked vegetables, vinegar, and parsley; serve.

Barley and mushroom risotto with Swiss chard

SERVES 6 TO 8

½ cup dried wild mushrooms

2 cups pearled barley

¼ cup unsalted butter, divided

3½ cups sliced mushroom caps

2 cups finely chopped peeled carrots (about 2 large)

2 cups finely chopped red onions (about 1 large)

3 tablespoons minced garlic

3 tablespoons tomato paste

3 tablespoons all-purpose flour

1 tablespoon Dijon mustard

1 cup red wine

3¾ cups low-sodium vegetable or chicken stock

1 cup canned diced tomatoes, with juice

1 tablespoon honey

2 teaspoons coarse salt

10 grinds black pepper

1 teaspoon dried thyme

½ teaspoon fennel seeds

2 dried bay leaves

2 cups torn Swiss chard leaves (stems removed)

¾ cup freshly grated Parmigiano-Reggiano

To convert this to a vegan dish, use olive oil and omit the butter and cheese; you might need more salt at the end.

1. In a small bowl, soak the dried mushrooms in about 2 cups boiling water for 30 minutes. Drain, reserving the soaking liquid. Mince the mushrooms and set aside. Pour the barley into the slow cooker.

2. Add half the butter to a medium-size, heavy saucepan and heat over medium high. When melted, add the sliced mushrooms, carrots, onions, and garlic. Sauté until the onions are softened and the mushrooms have released much of their liquid, about 11 minutes. Whisk in the tomato paste, flour, and mustard and cook until the flour disappears, about 1 minute.

3. Remove the pan from the heat, and add the wine; return the pan to the heat and raise the heat to high. Whisk, scraping up any browned bits in the pan, for 3 minutes. Add the rehydrated mushrooms and 1¼ cups soaking liquid, the stock, tomatoes, honey, salt, pepper, thyme, fennel seeds, and bay leaves; cook for 3 minutes. Pour the vegetable mixture over the barley, cover, and cook on low for 5 hours. Stir in the Swiss chard, re-cover, turn the heat to high, and cook until the barley is tender and the Swiss chard is cooked, about another 30 minutes. Remove the bay leaves, stir in the remaining 2 tablespoons butter and the cheese, and serve.

Cholent with apples and yams

SERVES 6

6 ounces dried chickpeas

1 yam, peeled and cut into eighths

3 large red potatoes, unpeeled and cut into four 1½- to 2-inch pieces

2 teaspoons coarse salt, divided

20 grinds black pepper, divided

⅓ cup all-purpose flour

1 teaspoon ground allspice

1⅔ pounds beef short ribs, in two pieces (ask the butcher to cut them for you)

2 tablespoons vegetable oil

½ cup raw pearled barley

1 apple, such as Granny Smith, peeled, cored, and cut into eighths

1 red onion, peeled, halved, and thinly sliced

1 white onion, peeled, halved, and thinly sliced

10 large cloves garlic

¼ cup tomato paste

1 cup red wine, such as Shiraz

1 cup low-sodium chicken or vegetable stock

2 tablespoons maple syrup

Here's an incredibly flavorful, Syrian-inspired take on a traditional Jewish dish. The wine brings this humble one-pot meal to a new level. Soak the dried chickpeas the night before preparing this dish, and remove the bones from the meat after cooking.

1. Soak the chickpeas in a bowl of water for at least 12 hours. Drain and pour 2 cups of the chickpeas into the bottom of the slow cooker. Place the yams and potatoes on top; sprinkle with 1 teaspoon salt and 10 grinds pepper.

2. In a large bowl, mix the flour with the remaining 1 teaspoon salt, remaining 10 grinds pepper, and the allspice. Add the beef and coat, reserving the excess flour. Heat the oil in a 10-inch, heavy frying pan over medium-high heat. When hot, add the meat and brown on both sides, about 10 minutes. Place on top of the potatoes. Sprinkle with the barley and top with the apples.

3. While the pan is still hot, add the red and white onions and garlic and sauté, stirring with a wooden spoon, until the onions are soft, about 4 minutes. Whisk in the tomato paste and reserved flour and cook until the flour is no longer visible, about 1 minute.

4. Remove the pan from the heat, add the wine, and return to the heat; raise the heat to high. Simmer, whisking, for 2 minutes. Add the stock and syrup and cook, whisking, for 2 minutes longer. Pour in the slow cooker and submerge the solids.

5. Cover and cook on low until the short ribs and potatoes are tender, about 10 hours. Remove the bones and serve.

Pork shoulder roast with fall vegetables, mustard, and capers

SERVES 6

4 red potatoes, unpeeled and quartered

2¼ cups 1½- to 2-inch pieces peeled parsnips (2 to 3 large)

2 cups 1½- to 2-inch cubes trimmed kohlrabi (about ⅔ pound or 2½ small bulbs)

2½ teaspoons coarse salt, divided

30 grinds black pepper, divided

2 teaspoons caraway seeds

2 teaspoons fennel seeds

½ cup finely chopped bread-and-butter pickles

5 tablespoons capers, rinsed and drained

3 tablespoons yellow mustard

One 3½-pound bone-in pork shoulder roast, trimmed of excess fat

3 tablespoons unsalted butter

2¼ cups finely chopped white onions (about 2 medium)

7 cloves garlic

3 tablespoons all-purpose flour

1 cup mild beer, such as Corona

3 tablespoons cider vinegar

1 cup low-sodium chicken stock

¼ cup apple juice

1 tablespoon honey

Garnish this flavorful, German-inspired dish with garlic breadcrumbs, which will give it some added flavor as well as crunch. Make sure the pork roast fits in your slow cooker, and ask your butcher to trim it of excess fat before weighing it (if you trim the meat yourself, you'll need a sharp boning knife, as the fat is quite thick). If you have time, toast the caraway and fennel seeds in a dry frying pan before grinding them to intensify their flavors.

If you can't find kohlrabi, swap in turnips, rutabagas, or carrots.

1. Place the potatoes, parsnips, kohlrabi, 1 teaspoon salt, and 12 grinds of pepper in the slow cooker. Toss well.

2. In a spice grinder, grind the caraway and fennel seeds. In a large bowl, mix together these ground spices, plus 1 teaspoon salt, 10 grinds of pepper, the pickles, capers, and mustard. Add the pork and coat all over with this mixture. Place the pork and any remaining rub on top of the vegetables.

3. Heat the butter in a 10-inch, heavy frying pan over medium-high heat. When melted, add the onions and garlic and sauté until the onions are softened, about 3 minutes. Whisk in the flour and cook until it is no longer visible, about 1 minute.

4. Remove the pan from the heat and add the beer and vinegar. Then return the pan to the heat, raise the heat to high, and whisk the mixture. Cook for 3 minutes, then whisk in the stock, juice, honey, and remaining ½ teaspoon salt and 8 grinds pepper. Cook for 2 minutes and pour over the pork. Cover and cook on low until the meat and vegetables are tender, 10 to 12 hours. Serve.

KOHLRABI

Also called stem or turnip cabbage, kohlrabi has a turniplike flavor. Look for firm, heavy stems and vibrantly colored greens, and store in the fridge for up to a week (longer if you remove the thin stems and leaves). Kohlrabi bulbs (simply enlarged, turnip-shaped stems) can be grated raw and tossed into coleslaws and salads or sliced and stir-fried, steamed, sautéed, or braised. The leaves are edible and can be sautéed for a vitamin-rich side.

Chicken with paprika, potatoes, and rosemary

SERVES 4

⅓ cup plus 3 tablespoons all-purpose flour, divided

8 bone-in, skinless chicken thighs (about 3 pounds)

2 teaspoons coarse salt, divided

2 teaspoons ground paprika, divided

6 cups 1-inch-diameter or larger red potatoes, each quartered (about 2 pounds)

¼ cup plus 1 tablespoon vegetable oil, divided

2 yellow onions, halved and sliced into ½-inch-thick rings

10 whole cloves garlic

2 tablespoons tomato paste

1 tablespoon plus 1 teaspoon Dijon mustard

½ cup white wine, such as Sauvignon Blanc

1 cup low-sodium chicken stock

1 teaspoon honey

1 bunch fresh rosemary sprigs, tied together with kitchen twine

This homey, comforting, rustic dish was inspired by the cooking of my husband's Hungarian grandmother, Yolanda ("Savta" to us). It's very simple and extremely crowd-pleasing. I jazzed up the Eastern European flavors with some fresh rosemary. Since the entrée contains potatoes, it's truly a one-pot meal.

1. Add ⅓ cup flour to a large bowl and dredge the chicken, shaking off and reserving the excess. Sprinkle the chicken all over with 1 teaspoon each of the salt and paprika. In another large bowl, toss the potatoes with the remaining 1 teaspoon each of salt and paprika, and add to the slow cooker.

2. Heat 2 tablespoons oil in a 10-inch, heavy sauté pan over medium-high heat. When hot, add half of the chicken and cook, turning over halfway through, until lightly golden brown on both sides, about 6 minutes. Place on top of the potatoes in the slow cooker. Repeat with another 1 tablespoon of the oil and the remaining chicken, about another 5 minutes, then add to the slow cooker.

3. Add 1 tablespoon oil, the onions, and garlic to the sauté pan. Sauté, breaking up the onion rings, until the onions are softened, about 4 minutes. Place over the chicken in the slow cooker. Add the remaining 1 tablespoon oil, 3 tablespoons flour, tomato paste, and mustard, and cook, stirring well, until the flour is no longer visible, about 30 seconds. Remove the pan from the heat, add the wine, then return

continued

the pan to high heat and bring to a boil. Boil for 1 minute, whisking. Then add the stock and honey and boil for another 3 minutes, whisking until almost smooth. Pour over the onions, chicken, and potatoes and nestle in the rosemary. Cover and cook on low until the chicken is tender, 4 hours.

4. Remove the rosemary, transfer the chicken and vegetables into a large, shallow serving dish, and serve at the table.

BROWNING MEAT

Browning meat markedly boosts flavor, so spend the roughly 15 minutes it requires. Browning is particularly helpful when working with ground meat; blander meats, such as chicken, turkey, and pork; and meats with very mild sauces (say, just stock and garlic). Red meats with flavorful rubs or sauces typically don't require browning.

Since you'll have removed the skin, the chicken won't become as deep in color as if you'd left it on. To ensure that it does become sufficiently golden brown, don't crowd the pan (leaving insufficient space between pieces of meat results in steaming, rather than browning). If necessary, brown the meat in batches. Turn it over roughly halfway through cooking so both sides develop color and flavor.

Braised chicken with brandy, bacon, and autumn vegetables

SERVES 6

6 whole bone-in, skinless chicken legs (scant 4½ pounds)

½ cup plus 1 tablespoon all-purpose flour

1¼ teaspoons coarse salt, divided

14 grinds black pepper, divided

¼ teaspoon ground nutmeg

12 ounces center-cut, uncured smokehouse bacon, cut into ½-inch pieces (about 2 cups)

4½ cups ½-inch diced peeled celeriac (about 1)

1¾ cups ½-inch slices peeled carrots (about 6 small)

1 yellow onion, halved and cut into ½-inch-thick slices

6 cloves garlic

2 tablespoons tomato paste

¾ cup brandy

1 cup low-sodium chicken stock

1 teaspoon honey

1½ pounds Brussels sprouts, halved and cores cut out (about 4½ cups)

1 tablespoon unsalted butter

1¼ pounds cremini mushrooms, de-stemmed and quartered

Inspired by coq au vin, this colorful fall dish balances the earthiness of mushrooms, bittersweet notes of Brussels sprouts, and smokiness of bacon. Feel free to use any type of mushroom. If you don't eat pork, omit the bacon—just swap in oil or butter to cook the chicken and use a bit more salt.

1. In a large bowl, coat the chicken with the flour, shaking off and reserving the excess. Sprinkle the chicken all over with a total of 1 teaspoon of the salt, 10 grinds of the pepper, and the nutmeg. Place the bacon in a single layer in a cold, 10-inch, heavy sauté pan. Heat over medium and cook until most of the fat renders, about 9 minutes. Raise the heat to medium high and cook until golden brown and a bit crisp, stirring, about 6 minutes. Transfer the bacon to the slow cooker (don't leave any bacon bits in the pan).

2. Add half of the chicken to the hot pan and cook until lightly golden brown on both sides, about 10 minutes. Repeat with the remaining chicken, about another 5 minutes. Transfer to a large plate. Pour all but about 2 tablespoons of the bacon

continued

fat into a small bowl and reserve. Add the celeriac, carrots, onions, and garlic to the hot pan, and cook, stirring, until slightly softened, about 7 minutes. Transfer the vegetables to the slow cooker and top with the chicken.

3. Add another tablespoon of bacon fat plus the tomato paste and any remaining flour to the sauté pan. Cook, stirring, until no flour is visible, about 30 seconds. Remove the pan from the heat, carefully add the brandy, then return the pan to the heat and bring to a boil over high heat. Boil, whisking, until the sauce is smooth and a bit thick, about 2 minutes. Stir in the stock and honey, and cook for another 2 minutes, whisking, until the sauce is smooth. Pour over the chicken. Cover and cook on low until the chicken is tender, 4 to 4½ hours.

4. Meanwhile, bring a covered pot of heavily salted water to a boil. When boiling, add the Brussels sprouts and cook over high heat until they're tender but still have a slight bite, about 7 minutes. Set aside. Heat 2 tablespoons of the bacon fat and the butter in a 10-inch, heavy sauté pan over medium-high heat. When the butter is melted, add the mushrooms, the remaining ¼ teaspoon salt, and 4 grinds pepper, and sauté until browned and tender, about 9 minutes.

5. Remove the chicken from the slow cooker, mix in the cooked vegetables (let them sit in the slow cooker for about 10 minutes if they've cooled), and add back in the chicken. Serve.

SPOTLIGHT ON

CELERIAC

Also known as celery root, celeriac is a mild, brown root vegetable that tastes of celery and parsley. Look for small, firm specimens, and store them loosely wrapped in the fridge's vegetable bin for 1 to 2 weeks. When ready to use, peel, then soak in lemon water (before cooking) to prevent discoloration. Grate or julienne raw celeriac for salads (I love it tossed with a mayonnaise-based dressing). Or, try celery root boiled and mashed with potatoes or simmered in soups and stews.

■ **PREP TIME:** About 1 hour ■ **SLOW COOKER TIME:** About 6 hours

Pork, chestnut, and parsnip ragu

SERVES 8 TO 10

2 slices white sandwich bread

½ cup whole milk

3 pounds ground pork

2 teaspoons coarse salt

15 grinds black pepper

½ teaspoon ground nutmeg

2 tablespoons unsalted butter

3¼ cups small-diced white onions (about 2)

3¼ cups small-diced peeled parsnips (3 to 4 large)

¾ cup small-diced celery (about 2 stalks)

2 tablespoons plus ½ teaspoon minced garlic

3 tablespoons tomato paste

3 tablespoons all-purpose flour

1 cup white wine, such as Chardonnay

One 14-ounce can peeled whole tomatoes, with juice

1 cup low-sodium chicken stock

½ cup fresh-squeezed orange juice (about 2 juicy oranges)

1 tablespoon light brown sugar

4 sprigs fresh sage, tied together with kitchen twine

1 cup coarsely chopped peeled and cooked chestnuts

Zest of 1 large navel orange

1 to 2 pounds pappardelle pasta, cooked according to the package directions

Freshly grated Parmigiano-Reggiano (optional)

Chestnuts add sweetness to this earthy, chunky meat sauce, which is best served over pappardelle pasta (the wide noodles help hold a lot of the sauce).

1. In a large bowl, mash together the bread and milk to form a paste. Add the pork, salt, pepper, and nutmeg, and gently knead together until well combined.

2. Add the butter to a medium-size, heavy saucepan and melt over medium-high heat. Add the onions, parsnips, celery, and garlic, and sauté until the onions are softened, about 8 minutes. Add the meat mixture and cook until browned a bit, breaking it up with a wooden spoon, about 15 minutes.

3. Add the tomato paste and flour and cook until the flour disappears, about 1 minute. Remove the pan from the heat and add the wine, then return to the heat and raise the heat to high. Cook for 2 minutes, then add the tomatoes, stock, orange juice, brown sugar, and sage. Cook for another 8 minutes, mashing the tomatoes a bit. Pour into the slow cooker. Cover and cook on low until the meat is cooked through and the sauce is flavorful, about 6 hours. Let the sauce sit for a minute, then use a large spoon or ladle to skim the fat off the surface (there will be a good amount).

4. Remove and discard the sage. Stir in the chestnuts and zest, and serve over the pasta, garnishing with cheese if desired.

SPOTLIGHT ON

CHESTNUTS

Nutty, sweet, and buttery, chestnuts are delicious in both sweet and savory dishes. If you buy them fresh, you'll need to remove their hard dark brown shells and bitter inner skins, which takes some time. Score each chestnut on its flat side. Then place on a baking sheet and roast in a 350°F oven for 15 to 20 minutes, until the nuts are aromatic and the shell and inner pellicle begin to split; peel. Alternatively, place in a saucepan, cover with water, and boil over medium-high heat until tender, about 20 minutes, then peel.

Sweet squash with cucumber-yogurt and tomato meat sauces

SERVES 4 TO 6

FOR THE SQUASH

3 cups low-sodium chicken stock

¾ cup plus 2 tablespoons granulated sugar

¼ cup fresh-squeezed, strained lemon juice

1 tablespoon red curry (not chile) paste

2 teaspoons coarse salt

1 teaspoon ground cinnamon

5 grinds black pepper

10½ cups 1½-inch chunks peeled butternut squash (from about 3 very large) or pumpkin

FOR THE MEAT SAUCE

2 tablespoons extra-virgin olive oil

1¼ pounds ground beef chuck

1 cup finely chopped white onions (about ½ large)

2 tablespoons minced garlic

2 tablespoons tomato paste

One 28-ounce can tomato purée

1 tablespoon granulated sugar

1 teaspoon coarse salt

½ teaspoon crushed dried mint leaves

5 grinds black pepper

FOR THE YOGURT SAUCE

2 cups plus 2 tablespoons Greek yogurt (not low fat)

1 scant cup coarsely grated English cucumber (about 1)

¼ cup finely chopped fresh mint leaves

1 tablespoon minced garlic

1 teaspoon salt

1 teaspoon granulated sugar

10 grinds black pepper

This entrée is based on a traditional Afghani recipe, but the squash is so sweet that it can also be served as dessert with ice cream or crème anglaise.

Although pumpkin is authentic, I use butternut squash for convenience. To save time, prepare the yogurt and meat sauces in advance, and simply heat up the meat sauce before serving.

MAKE THE SQUASH
In the slow cooker, stir together the first seven ingredients. Add the squash and mix well, submerging in the liquid. Cover and cook on low until tender but not falling apart, about 5 hours.

MAKE THE MEAT SAUCE

Add the oil to a medium-size, heavy saucepan and heat over medium high. When hot, add the meat and cook until almost all browned, about 7 minutes. Add the onions, garlic, and tomato paste, and cook until the onions are softened, about 3 minutes. Add the tomato purée, sugar, salt, mint, and pepper, and bring to a boil over high heat. Cover and reduce the heat to low. Simmer until the flavors meld, about 15 minutes.

MAKE THE YOGURT SAUCE

Stir together all of the ingredients in a medium-size bowl. Refrigerate until serving.

TO SERVE

Spoon yogurt sauce into serving bowls. Top with chunks of squash and a ladleful of warm meat sauce.

Bolognese sauce with pancetta, porcini, and rosemary

MAKES 11 CUPS

¼ cup dried porcini or other wild mushrooms

3 slices white bread

1 cup whole milk

Scant 3 pounds ground beef chuck or meatloaf mix, at room temperature

2 teaspoons coarse salt

15 grinds black pepper

2 tablespoons unsalted butter

½ pound pancetta, coarsely chopped

1 cup finely chopped porcini mushrooms (about 5 large)

2 cups finely chopped carrots (about 4 medium)

1 cup finely chopped celery (about 4 stalks)

1 cup finely chopped red onions (about 1 small)

1 tablespoon finely chopped garlic

1 teaspoon ground nutmeg

½ cup tomato paste (about 5 ounces)

¼ cup all-purpose flour

1 cup dry red wine, such as Cabernet Sauvignon,

¾ cup canned diced tomatoes, with juice

½ cup low-sodium chicken stock

2 tablespoons minced fresh rosemary leaves

1 pound pappardelle pasta, cooked according to the package directions

This rich, complex sauce smells and tastes like fall—with its earthy mushrooms, smoky pancetta, and sweet woodsy rosemary. Serve it over pasta, ideally pappardelle, and freeze any extra (this recipe makes a lot of sauce). I use a smaller quantity of milk than is traditional, since milk can curdle in the slow cooker. Be sure to use high-quality pancetta and feel free to vary the kind of mushroom.

1. Add the dried mushrooms to a small bowl and cover with very hot water; let sit for 15 minutes, then drain and finely chop. In a large bowl, mash the bread and milk together until a smooth paste forms. Gently knead in the beef, salt, and pepper, and mix well.

2. Add the butter to a medium-size, heavy saucepan and heat over medium-high heat. When melted, add the pancetta and sauté until browned, about 8 minutes. Pour off all but about 2 tablespoons of the fat. Add the meat mixture, and cook until browned, about 10 minutes. Add the fresh porcini and cook until softened, about 2 minutes. Stir in the dried mushrooms, carrots, celery, onions, garlic, and nutmeg.

continued

Sauté until the vegetables are slightly softened and aromatic, about 3 minutes. Add the tomato paste and flour, and cook until the flour is no longer visible, no more than 1 minute. With the pan off the heat, carefully add the wine. Then return the pan to high heat and stir well, scraping the bottom of the pan with a wooden spoon to release any food bits. Cook for 2 minutes, then stir in the tomatoes and stock, and cook for another minute. Pour into the slow cooker.

3. Cover the slow cooker and cook on low until the meat has cooked through and the sauce is aromatic and very flavorful, about 6 hours. Spoon the fat off the surface, stir in the rosemary, break up the meat more with a fork, and serve with pasta.

SLOW COOKER SECRET

DETERMINING ACCOMPANIMENTS

When deciding on accompaniments to the recipes, rely on the suggestions I've provided in the headnotes as well as on traditional pairings, like Bolognese sauce with pappardelle pasta or vegetable chili with tortilla chips. Classic stews, such as pot roast, are delicious spooned over or alongside starches, but don't rely on the old standbys. Instead, try polenta, rice, couscous, quinoa, farro, pasta, mashed root vegetables, or toasts. And don't forget a quickly cooked fresh vegetable, which rounds out the plate. Top desserts with ice cream, crème fraîche, sweetened sour cream, whipped cream, or sweet sauces.

Thai tofu, Swiss chard, and sweet potato curry

SERVES 6 TO 8

24 ounces extra-firm unflavored tofu

¼ cup plus 3 tablespoons dark brown sugar

¼ cup plus 3 tablespoons red curry (not chile) paste

6 cups 1-inch-diced peeled sweet potatoes (about 2 large)

1 teaspoon coarse salt

5 grinds black pepper

2 to 3 tablespoons vegetable oil, divided

2 tablespoons peeled grated fresh ginger

2 tablespoons minced lemongrass stalk (from the light part only)

2 tablespoons minced garlic

¼ cup all-purpose flour

One 13½-ounce can full-fat coconut milk

½ cup canned pumpkin

¼ cup fresh-squeezed, strained lime juice

¼ cup low-sodium vegetable or chicken stock

½ bunch Swiss chard, stems removed and leaves sliced ¼ inch thick, then chopped crosswise (about 2 cups packed)

Serve this creamy, rich aromatic stew over brown rice; to jazz things up, enrich the grains with butter and lime zest. Since different brands of curry paste feature different levels of salt and heat, taste and adjust the seasoning accordingly. Instead of vegetable oil, you could use coconut oil, unsalted butter, or peanut oil. For ease, buy prechopped sweet potatoes and feel free to skip the fresh ginger, lemongrass, and garlic.

1. Place two layers of paper towels on a plate, then top with the tofu, then another two layers of paper towels, and a large plate. Leave for about 15 minutes to drain. Cut the tofu into 1-inch cubes. In a small bowl, stir together the brown sugar and curry paste. Add one-third of this mixture to a zip-top, gallon-size plastic bag. Add the tofu and gently coat it with the marinade, using your hands to massage it. Close the bag and refrigerate.

2. Pour the potatoes into the slow cooker, then mix with another third of the sugar-curry mixture and all of the salt and pepper. Heat 2 tablespoons of oil in a 10-inch, heavy sauté pan over medium-high heat. When hot, add the ginger, lemongrass,

continued

and garlic, and sauté until softened, about 2 minutes. Add the final third of the sugar-curry mixture, plus the flour (and the remaining 1 tablespoon of oil if the pan is very dry), and cook, stirring, until no white flour is visible, no more than a minute. Add the coconut milk, pumpkin, lime juice, and stock, and bring to a boil over high heat, whisking vigorously to remove any lumps. Cook until smooth, thickened, and some bubbles appear, about 4 minutes. Pour over the potatoes.

3. Cover the slow cooker and cook on low until the potatoes are very tender but still retain their shape, about 4 hours. Stir in the chard and marinated tofu, cover, and cook on high until the chard is tender, about another 20 minutes. Serve immediately.

SPOTLIGHT ON

SWISS CHARD

Chard, a member of the beet family, is a hardy green with crinkly leaves and firm, fairly wide stems. It comes in several varieties; most beautiful is rainbow chard, whose stalks feature many colors.

To prepare chard, cut off and discard the thick stems. Or cut them off, thinly slice them, and cook them for longer than the leaves. The leaves should be thinly sliced, also known as cut into chiffonade. Store in the fridge and use within a few days.

Turkey stew with yams, carrots, and apples

SERVES 8

5 cups 1½- to 2-inch chunks peeled yams (or sweet potatoes)

3 cups peeled and cored apple wedges, such as Granny Smith

1 cup 1½- to 2-inch chunks peeled carrots (about 1 large)

2 teaspoons coarse salt, divided

16 grinds black pepper, divided

¼ cup plus 2 tablespoons all-purpose flour

1 teaspoon dried sage

1 teaspoon dried thyme

¼ teaspoon ground ginger

3¾ pounds boneless, skinless turkey thighs (about 4 thighs)

2 tablespoons unsalted butter

1 tablespoon vegetable oil

2 cups coarsely chopped red onions (about 1 large)

1 cup plus 3 tablespoons coarsely chopped celery

3 large cloves garlic

2 tablespoons Dijon mustard

1 cup apple juice

1 cup low-sodium chicken stock

This aromatic stew is an inexpensive, fun variation on the classic Thanksgiving turkey dinner since it features all the elements of the traditional holiday meal. With a highly flavorful broth, it would be ideal served in shallow soup bowls. Try it with biscuits on the side or dumplings cooked in the broth.

Since turkey thighs are so large, each one serves two; just cut the meat into eight pieces before serving. Be sure to call the store before picking up the turkey thighs; they can be difficult to find outside the Thanksgiving holiday season.

1. In the bottom of a slow cooker, toss the yams, apples, carrots, 1 teaspoon salt, and 8 grinds pepper.

2. In a large bowl, mix together the flour, sage, thyme, ginger, and remaining 1 teaspoon salt and 8 grinds pepper. Add the turkey thighs and coat with the flour, shaking off and reserving any excess.

3. Heat the butter in a 10-inch, heavy sauté pan over medium-high heat. When melted and hot, add half of the turkey and cook on both sides until golden brown, about 6 minutes total, then place on top of the yam-apple mixture in the slow cooker. Add the oil and remaining turkey to the sauté pan and repeat, about another 4 minutes; transfer to the slow cooker.

4. While the pan is still hot, add the onions, celery, and garlic, and sauté until the onions are softened, about 5 minutes. Whisk in the reserved flour and the mustard and cook until the flour disappears, about 1 minute. Add the juice and stock and raise the heat to high. Cook, whisking, for 5 minutes, then pour on top of the turkey. Cover and cook on low until the meat and yams are tender, 5 to 7 hours. Serve.

SLOW COOKER SECRET

CUSTOMIZING DISHES FOR SPECIAL DIETS

Many recipes in this book are vegetarian, vegan, or kosher. However, to convert more dishes to your lifestyle, always assume that you can substitute low-sodium vegetable broth or water for chicken broth. In some dishes—such as chili—feel free to substitute the meat with beans. And if you don't eat pork, you can substitute another kind of meat. Similarly, turkey bacon, chicken sausage, or vegetarian sausage can stand in for bacon and sausage. Replace butter with oil or a trans-fat-free butter substitute.

You can also use intensely flavored ingredients, such as smoked paprika, chipotle chile in adobo sauce, dried wild mushrooms, or seaweed to compensate for some of the salty, smoky punch of meat products, such as bacon.

If a suggested garnish is sour cream and you're vegan, substitute nondairy yogurt. If you don't drink, swap in cider or apricot nectar for beer or wine.

In all cases, read the recipe and make sure the flavor of the ingredient substitute jibes with the dish. You'll likely need to taste the dish and adjust the flavors before serving.

■ **PREP TIME:** About 1½ hours, including making the dumpling batter
■ **SLOW COOKER TIME:** 4 to 4½ hours

Chorizo and kale stew with cornmeal dumplings

SERVES 6

1½ teaspoons coarse salt, plus more for cooking the kale

9 cups torn fresh kale leaves (stems removed)

3 tablespoons unsalted butter, divided

2 pounds fresh (raw) chorizo sausages (about 10), left whole

1 cup finely chopped red onions (about ½ large)

1 cup finely chopped celery (about 2 large stalks)

1 cup finely chopped peeled carrots (1 to 2 large)

1 cup finely chopped red bell pepper (1 to 2)

2 tablespoons sliced scallions, white and light green parts only

2 tablespoons minced garlic

5 grinds black pepper

¼ teaspoon ground cayenne pepper

¼ cup tomato paste

⅔ cup plus 3 tablespoons all-purpose flour, divided

2 tablespoons Dijon mustard

1 cup mild beer, such as Corona

¼ cup cider vinegar

One 14½-ounce can fire-roasted diced tomatoes

1 cup low-sodium chicken stock

2 tablespoons mild honey

⅓ cup yellow cornmeal

2 teaspoons packed light brown sugar

1 teaspoon baking powder

½ cup 2% or whole milk

Cajun and Southern cuisine inspired this colorful dish. Use fresh, raw Mexican chorizo (rather than dried Spanish chorizo), and be sure to squeeze out excess water from the kale to avoid a watery stew. Feel free to substitute other hardy greens if you don't like kale; collard greens would be a good choice. If you love dumplings (and who doesn't?!), double the dough for more servings.

1. Fill a medium saucepan two-thirds full of water, add plenty of salt, and bring to a boil. Once boiling, add the kale and cook for 1 minute. Rinse with cold water, drain, and squeeze out any remaining water. Set aside.

2. Place 2 tablespoons of butter in a 10-inch, heavy, frying pan and heat over medium high. When melted and hot, add half of the chorizo and cook until golden brown, about 5 minutes. Transfer to the slow cooker. Add the remaining chorizo and brown, about another 5 minutes. Transfer to the slow cooker, then add the kale.

3. While the pan is still hot, add the onions, celery, carrots, bell peppers, scallions, garlic, 1 teaspoon salt, the pepper, and cayenne. Cook, stirring with a wooden spoon, until the onions are softened, about 5 minutes.

4. Whisk in the tomato paste, 3 tablespoons of flour, and mustard, and whisk until the flour is no longer visible, about 1 minute. Remove the pan from the heat, add the beer and vinegar, and then return to the heat and raise the heat to high. Simmer, whisking, for 3 minutes. Add the tomatoes, stock, and honey, and cook for another 2 minutes. Pour over the kale and chorizo in the slow cooker, submerging them in the liquid. Cover and cook on low until the chorizo is cooked and the greens are tender, 3 to 3½ hours.

5. Meanwhile, in a medium bowl, whisk together the remaining ⅔ cup flour, the cornmeal, brown sugar, baking powder, and remaining ½ teaspoon salt. With your hands, gently mix in the remaining 1 tablespoon of butter, then the milk (the dough will be sticky). Shape into six balls. Uncover the slow cooker and place the dumplings evenly on top of the greens. Re-cover and cook on high until the dumplings are cooked through, about 1 hour. Serve, spooning one dumpling into each serving bowl.

SPOTLIGHT ON

KALE

Kale, a member of the cabbage family, is a hardy green with frilly, deep-hued leaves. Look for a vibrant green color—no yellow—and firm, not limp leaves. Cut off and discard the thick kale stems, thinly slice or chiffonade the leaves, and cook or serve raw in salads. Store in the fridge and use within a couple of days.

Braised bratwurst with apples and beer

SERVES 5

2 tablespoons unsalted butter

2¼ pounds fresh (raw) bratwurst (about 10 links)

3 apples, such as Granny Smith, peeled, cored, and cut into eighths

2 cups finely chopped red onions (about 1 large onion)

½ cup finely chopped celery (1 to 2 large stalks)

2 tablespoons minced garlic

3 tablespoons all-purpose flour

2 tablespoons spicy brown mustard

1 cup beer

1 cup apple juice

½ cup prepared sauerkraut

½ teaspoon coarse salt

10 grinds black pepper

Inspired by German cuisine, this stew features tender bratwurst and apples that melt into the flavorful sauce. Ladle it into shallow bowls, and serve with brown bread slathered with butter and sprinkled with sea salt. Be sure to use fresh (raw) bratwurst rather than the previously cooked type. If you don't eat pork, substitute chicken or turkey sausage.

1. Place the butter in a 10-inch, heavy type frying pan and heat over medium high. When melted and hot, add the brats and brown in two batches, about 9 minutes total. Transfer to the slow cooker. Place the apples on top of the bratwurst.

2. Add the onions, celery, and garlic to the hot pan, and sauté, stirring with a wooden spoon, until the onions are softened, about 4 minutes. Whisk in the flour and mustard, and cook until the flour is no longer visible, about 1 minute.

3. Remove the pan from the heat and add the beer, then return it to the heat and raise the heat to high. Cook, whisking, for 2 minutes. Add the juice, sauerkraut, salt, and pepper, and cook for another 2 minutes. Pour over the bratwurst and apples in the slow cooker, pushing down the solids to submerge in the liquid.

4. Cover and cook on low until the bratwurst and apples are tender and cooked through, about 5 hours. Serve.

Spiced chicken with chickpeas, carrots, and Swiss chard

SERVES 3 TO 4

One 15-ounce can chickpeas, rinsed and drained

¼ cup all-purpose flour

1 teaspoon cumin

1 teaspoon ground coriander

⅛ teaspoon ground cayenne

6 bone-in, skinless chicken thighs (about 2 pounds)

2 tablespoons olive oil

2 cups coarsely chopped white onions (about 1 large)

1½ cups coarsely chopped peeled carrots (1 to 2 large)

6 large cloves garlic

½ teaspoon coarse salt

8 grinds black pepper

1 cup low-sodium chicken stock

¼ cup fresh-squeezed, strained lemon juice

2 tablespoons honey

3½ cups packed coarsely chopped Swiss chard leaves, stems removed (about ⅔ pound)

This delicious, vibrant, healthful stew features Middle Eastern flavors: cumin, coriander, and cayenne. Easy to prepare, it's best served immediately after cooking so the chard doesn't get stringy.

1. Pour the chickpeas into the bottom of the slow cooker.

2. In a large bowl, mix together the flour with the cumin, coriander, and cayenne. Add the chicken and coat with the flour, shaking off and reserving the excess flour.

3. Heat the oil in a 10-inch, heavy sauté pan over medium-high heat. When hot, add the chicken and cook in two batches until golden brown on both sides, about 10 minutes total. Place the chicken on top of the chickpeas.

4. Add the onions, carrots, garlic, salt, and pepper to the pan and sauté until the onions are softened, about 5 minutes. Whisk in the reserved flour and cook until the flour disappears, about 1 minute. Add the stock, juice, and honey, and raise the heat to high. Cook for 3 minutes, then pour over the chicken. Cover and cook on low until the chicken is tender, about 4½ hours.

5. Stir in the Swiss chard leaves, submerging them as much as possible in the liquid. Raise the heat to high, re-cover, and cook until the greens are tender, another 30 to 45 minutes. Serve.

Chicken and peanut stew with butternut squash and kale

SERVES 4 TO 6

⅓ cup plus 1 tablespoon all-purpose flour

2½ teaspoons coarse salt, divided, plus more for cooking the kale

½ teaspoon ground ginger

5 grinds black pepper

⅛ teaspoon crushed red pepper flakes

2⅔ pounds bone-in, skinless chicken thighs (about 6 thighs)

¼ cup peanut oil

5 cups finely chopped peeled butternut squash (about 2)

2 cups finely chopped white onions (about 1 large)

1¾ cups finely chopped red bell peppers (about 1)

¾ cup finely chopped peeled carrots (1 to 2 large)

8 whole cloves garlic

1 tablespoon minced jalapeño (without seeds or membranes)

¼ cup tomato paste

3 tablespoons peanut butter (creamy or chunky)

2 tablespoons Dijon mustard

1 cup mild beer, such as Corona

½ cup low-sodium chicken stock

¼ cup honey

3 tablespoons cider vinegar

4 cups coarsely chopped kale leaves (about 1 large bunch)

½ cup unsalted peanuts, lightly toasted, chopped, and mixed with ¼ teaspoon coarse salt

Mild and colorful, this stew will appeal to adults and kids alike. Rich, meaty, salty peanuts contrast with the sweet squash and the green, slightly bitter kale for a satisfying dish.

1. In a large bowl, mix together the flour, 1 teaspoon of the salt, the ginger, black pepper, and red pepper flakes. Add the chicken and dredge, shaking off and reserving any remaining flour. Heat half of the oil in a medium-size, heavy saucepan over medium-high heat. When hot, add half of the chicken and cook on both sides until light golden brown, about 7 minutes; transfer to the slow cooker. Repeat with the remaining chicken, about another 7 minutes.

2. While the pan is still hot, add the remaining oil, the squash, onions, peppers, carrots, garlic, jalapeño, and the remaining 1½ teaspoons salt. Sauté, stirring, until the onions begin to soften, about 4 minutes. Stir in the reserved seasoned flour, tomato paste, peanut butter, and mustard. Cook until the flour is no longer visible, about 2 minutes. Remove the pan from the heat, add the beer, then return the pan to the heat and raise the heat to high. Cook for 3 minutes, then add the stock, honey, and vinegar. Cook for 3 minutes, and pour the mixture over the chicken. Cover and cook on low until the chicken is tender, about 4 hours.

3. Meanwhile, bring a medium-size, heavy saucepan two-thirds full of heavily salted water to a boil over high heat. Once boiling, add the kale and cook until tender, about 6 minutes. Drain and rinse with cold water. Stir into the finished stew, and serve each portion sprinkled with chopped peanuts.

SLOW COOKER SECRET

SKINNING CHICKEN

I remove the skin from chicken when slow-cooking since it would become limp and slimy if left on. It's cheaper to buy chicken with skin on and then remove it yourself. The easiest way to do this is to grip the flesh tightly in one hand while using your other hand to pull off the skin.

Shepherd's pie with a red wine, Cheddar, and root vegetable topping

SERVES 8 TO 10

2 slices white bread

2 cups whole milk, divided

2¼ pounds ground beef

2½ teaspoons coarse salt, divided (plus salt for cooking the potatoes)

18 grinds black pepper, divided

¼ cup unsalted butter, divided

2¼ cups finely chopped red onions (about 1 large)

2 cups finely chopped peeled carrots (about 2 large)

1 cup finely chopped peeled parsnips (about 3 small)

15 small cloves garlic, 8 left whole and 7 finely chopped (about 1 tablespoon), divided

¼ cup tomato paste

2 tablespoons all-purpose flour

1 cup red wine, such as Cabernet Sauvignon

One 28-ounce can whole peeled tomatoes, with juice

2 sprigs fresh rosemary

6¼ cups large chunks of peeled root vegetables, such as 3 russet potatoes, 1 small turnip, ¼ rutabaga, and ⅓ celery root

¼ teaspoon ground nutmeg

2½ cups sharp Cheddar cheese, coarsely grated (about ½ pound)

A variety of root vegetables presents a lovely, complex twist on a classic dish. Very rich and nutty from the Cheddar, this is perfect for company—but inexpensive. Finishing it in the oven melts the cheese and yields a golden, slightly crisp topping. To make it a bit lighter, you can drain off some of the fat from the meat mixture, cut the amount of cheese, and use 2% milk in the potato purée. For convenience, make the root vegetable topping in advance. If you have extra meat filling, serve it in hamburger buns for an elegant, autumnal take on sloppy Joes.

1. In a large bowl, mash together the bread and ½ cup of milk. Gently knead in the meat, 2 teaspoons of salt, and 10 grinds of pepper, mixing well. Heat half of the butter in a large, heavy saucepan over medium-high heat. When the butter has melted, add the meat-bread mixture, pushing down with a wooden spoon, and brown, 10 to 11 minutes. Add the onions, carrots, parsnips, and finely chopped garlic,

continued

and sauté until the onions have softened, about 3 minutes. Add the tomato paste and flour and stir until the flour disappears, about 1 minute. Remove the pan from the heat, add the wine, and then cook for 1 to 2 minutes, stirring. Add the tomatoes and rosemary and bring to a boil, about 2 minutes, gently mashing the tomatoes with a potato masher. Carefully pour into the slow cooker, cover, and cook on low until the flavors are blended together, 4 to 6 hours. Remove and discard the rosemary sprigs and—using a large ladle or spoon—skim the grease off the surface.

2. Meanwhile, place the root vegetable chunks in a medium-size saucepan, cover with cold water by about 2 inches, and salt generously. Bring to a boil over high heat, then cover and reduce to a simmer over medium low; simmer until very tender, about 15 minutes. Meanwhile, add the remaining 1½ cups milk, remaining garlic, the nutmeg, remaining 2 tablespoons butter, ½ teaspoon salt, and 8 grinds pepper to a small saucepan. Bring to a simmer over medium-high heat. Drain the root vegetables over a colander in the sink, then pour the root vegetables back into the dry pot. Mash with a potato masher, pouring in the milk mixture. Stir until a smooth purée forms.

3. Heat the oven to 400°F. Place a 9x13x2-inch baking dish on a rimmed baking sheet. Ladle the meat filling into the baking dish. Cover with the root vegetable mash, spreading evenly. Sprinkle evenly with cheese. Bake until the cheese melts, the potatoes turn golden brown, and the meat sauce thickens, 25 to 30 minutes. Serve.

SPOTLIGHT ON

RUTABAGAS

Large and pale yellow, rutabagas—members of the cabbage family—are not the most attractive root vegetables. However, they are earthy, nutty, and slightly sweet once peeled and cooked. At the grocery store, you should find them next to turnips, their kissing cousins. Look for firm, heavy vegetables, and store them unwashed in the fridge's vegetable bin for up to 2 weeks.

Greek-style winter squash, chickpea, and Swiss chard stew

SERVES 4 TO 6

2 dried bay leaves

3 tablespoons olive oil, divided

1¾ cups finely chopped red onions (about 1 large)

3 tablespoons minced garlic

8 cups 1½- to 2-inch cubes peeled butternut squash (1 very large)

1 teaspoon coarse salt

10 grinds black pepper

½ teaspoon dried thyme

½ teaspoon ground cinnamon

½ teaspoon dried dill

½ teaspoon dried mint

3 tablespoons tomato paste

2 tablespoons all-purpose flour

One 14-ounce can whole peeled tomatoes, with juice

1 cup low-sodium vegetable or chicken stock

¼ cup fresh-squeezed, strained lemon juice

1 tablespoon honey

3 cups coarsely chopped Swiss chard leaves (stems removed)

One 15½-ounce can chickpeas, rinsed and drained

½ cup golden raisins

Spoon this vegetarian stew over bulgur, couscous, or quinoa, and garnish with fresh mint or dill. To add oomph, crumble some feta or goat cheese over the top of each serving.

1. Place the bay leaves in the slow cooker.

2. Heat 2 tablespoons of oil in a 10-inch, heavy sauté pan over medium-high heat. When the pan is hot, add the onions and garlic and sauté until the onions are softened, about 3 minutes. Add the squash, salt, pepper, thyme, cinnamon, dill, and mint, and sauté, stirring with a wooden spoon, for 4 minutes. Pour into the slow cooker.

3. While the pan is still hot, stir in the remaining oil plus the tomato paste and flour, and whisk until the flour is no longer visible, no more than 1 minute. Add the tomatoes (with juices), stock, lemon juice, and honey, and raise the heat to high. Cook, whisking, until the sauce thickens, about 5 minutes. Pour over the squash in the slow cooker, submerging the squash.

4. Cover and cook on low until the squash is tender, about 3½ hours. Stir in the chard, chickpeas, and raisins; re-cover and raise the heat to high. Cook until the chard and squash are tender, about 30 minutes.

Turkey and butternut squash chili with apple-cilantro garnish

SERVES 8 TO 10

2 slices white bread

½ cup whole milk

1½ pounds ground turkey

1 cup canned pumpkin

1 cup canned diced tomatoes, with juice (about two-thirds of a 14.5-ounce can)

¼ cup apricot nectar or orange or apple juice

2 tablespoons fresh-squeezed, strained lime juice

¼ cup olive oil, divided

6 cups packed ½-inch-cubed peeled butternut squash (about 1 large)

1½ cups finely chopped red onions (about 1 large)

2 tablespoons minced garlic

2 teaspoons chili powder, divided

2 teaspoons coarse salt, divided

10 grinds black pepper, divided

2 tablespoons tomato paste

2 tablespoons liquid from a can of chipotle chiles en adobo

2 tablespoons all-purpose flour

One 15-ounce can white (cannellini) beans, drained and rinsed

One 15½-ounce can chickpeas, rinsed and drained

Apple-Cilantro Garnish, for serving (recipe on p. 206)

With its orange color, this slightly sweet, mild chili is ideal for Super Bowl parties or Halloween, and it will please adults and kids alike. For variation, you can use chicken instead of turkey thighs and different types of canned beans; to up the heat, add minced jalapeño or increase the chipotle. To save time, buy precut squash, garlic, and onions. Prepare the garnish—so delicious, you might want to double it—within a couple of hours of serving.

1. In a medium bowl, mash the bread and milk together until a smooth paste forms, then gently knead in the meat; set aside. In a small bowl, combine the pumpkin, tomatoes, nectar, and lime juice; set aside.

2. Heat half of the oil in a 10-inch, heavy sauté pan over medium-high heat. When hot, add the squash, onions, garlic, half of the chili powder, 1 teaspoon salt, and 5 grinds pepper. Sauté, stirring, until the mixture is aromatic and the squash is slightly softened when poked with a fork, about 6 minutes. Transfer to the slow cooker. *continued*

3. Add the remaining oil, meat-bread mixture, tomato paste, chipotle liquid, flour, remaining chili powder, salt, and pepper to the pan. Sauté, stirring with a wooden spoon, until aromatic and the flour is no longer visible, about 5 minutes. Add the pumpkin-nectar mix to the pan and simmer, stirring, for 2 more minutes. Add to the slow cooker. Mix in the beans and the chickpeas, cover, and cook on low until the meat is cooked through and the squash is tender, 4 to 6 hours. Serve with Apple-Cilantro Garnish on the side.

Apple-Cilantro Garnish

1¼ cups ⅓-inch-diced unpeeled sweet apples, such as Macintosh (about 2 medium)	¼ cup finely chopped fresh cilantro leaves 2 tablespoons fresh-squeezed, strained lime juice	⅛ teaspoon coarse salt 5 grinds black pepper

Spoon just a bit of this tart-sweet topping onto each portion of chili for a colorful garnish.

Mix the ingredients together in a small bowl, chill, and serve with the chili.

Beef, potato, and pumpkin stew with soy sauce and mirin

SERVES 6 TO 8

6 cups 1½-inch cubes peeled pumpkin or butternut squash

4 cups 1½-inch cubes peeled russet or Idaho potatoes

⅓ cup all-purpose flour

½ teaspoon coarse salt

10 grinds black pepper

2 pounds beef chuck cut into 1½- to 2-inch cubes

5 tablespoons vegetable oil, divided

2 cups finely chopped red onions (about 1 large)

1 cup sliced scallions, plus more for garnish

1 cup finely chopped peeled carrots (1 to 2)

2 tablespoons minced garlic

2 tablespoons tomato paste

½ teaspoon wasabi paste

½ cup mirin (sweetened sake)

2 cups low-sodium chicken stock

¼ cup plus 2 tablespoons reduced-sodium soy sauce

This stick-to-your-ribs stew is brimming with Japanese flavors. Serve it over white rice, and garnish with thinly sliced scallions. Mirin, a very sweet cooking wine, is available in the Asian section of the grocery store.

1. Place the pumpkin (or squash) and potatoes in the slow cooker.

2. Mix the flour, salt, and pepper in a large bowl. Add the beef and coat, shaking off and reserving the excess flour. Heat 2 tablespoons of the oil in a 10-inch, heavy frying pan over medium-high heat. When hot, add half of the beef and brown, about 7 minutes; transfer to the slow cooker. Add another 2 tablespoons of oil and the remaining beef and brown, about another 5 minutes; add to the slow cooker.

3. Add the remaining 1 tablespoon oil and the onions, scallions, carrots, and garlic to the hot pan and sauté until the onions are softened, about 5 minutes. Whisk in the tomato paste, wasabi paste, and reserved flour, and cook until no more white flour is visible, about 30 seconds.

4. Remove the pan from the heat and add the mirin. Return the pan to the heat, raise the heat to high, and cook, whisking, for 2 minutes. Add the stock and soy sauce and cook for another 3 minutes. Pour over the meat-pumpkin mixture in the slow cooker and use a spoon to submerge the solids in the liquids.

5. Cover and cook on low until the beef is fork-tender and the vegetables are cooked through, about 7½ hours. Serve, garnishing with extra scallions.

Sticky toffee pudding with cranberries

SERVES 8

About 1 tablespoon unsalted butter, at room temperature, for the dish

FOR THE SAUCE

2 cups heavy cream

½ cup dark brown sugar

½ cup golden syrup (such as Lyle's) or molasses

1 cup fresh (or frozen, thawed, and drained) cranberries, picked over

⅛ teaspoon coarse salt

FOR THE PUDDING

4 ounces pitted dates, chopped (about ½ cup plus 1 tablespoon packed)

2 ounces sweetened dried cranberries (⅓ cup packed)

1 teaspoon baking soda

1¼ cups all-purpose flour

1 teaspoon baking powder

1 tablespoon espresso powder

½ teaspoon coarse salt

½ stick unsalted butter, at room temperature

¾ cup granulated sugar

2 large eggs, at room temperature

1 teaspoon vanilla bean paste or pure vanilla extract

crème fraîche or vanilla ice cream, for serving (optional)

This pièce-de-résistance dessert is ideal for Thanksgiving, Christmas, and other cold-weather holidays. To the much-loved British classic, I've added seasonal fresh and dried cranberries; the former dot the rich sauce, like red Christmas ornaments. To gild the lily further, serve with crème fraîche or vanilla ice cream. Be sure to use Lyle's Golden Syrup, which tastes just like rich caramel sauce.

Feel free to complete Step 2 the day before serving, chilling the sauce in the fridge instead of the freezer and reheating the sauce in the microwave or on the stove right before pouring over the pudding. Make sure your baking dish fits in your slow cooker; my Pillivuyt 10½- x 7½- x 2-inch (1.5-quart) oval baking dish is the perfect size. See p. 211 for more information.

1. Grease a 1½-quart, deep oval baking dish (or one that will fit in your slow cooker) with the butter.

2. Meanwhile, add all of the sauce ingredients to a heavy, medium-size saucepan, and bring to a boil over medium-high heat. Cook, stirring frequently, until the mixture is thickened and the cranberries are cooked, about 10 minutes (watch, as you don't want

continued

the mixture to boil over). Pour half of this sauce into the baking dish, and place the dish in the freezer until the mixture solidifies. (Refrigerate the remaining sauce, then warm in a small saucepan over medium-low heat when ready to serve.)

3. Wash out the medium saucepan, then add the dates, dried cranberries, and 1 cup of water, and bring to a low boil over high heat. Remove from the heat and immediately mix in the baking soda (the mixture will foam a bit). In a small bowl, whisk together the flour, baking powder, espresso powder, and salt. In a stand mixer (or a large bowl with a hand mixer), beat the butter and granulated sugar on medium-high speed until light and fluffy, about 5 minutes. Slowly beat in the eggs and vanilla, scraping down the sides of the bowl with a rubber spatula to incorporate everything. Beat on medium-high speed for a couple of minutes to mix well. Reduce the speed to low, then beat in half of the flour mixture, then the date mixture. On low speed, beat in the remaining flour mixture until just combined (do not overmix). Remove the baking dish from the freezer. Pour the batter on top of the solidified cranberry mixture, and cover tightly with foil.

4. Place a trivet or small rack (or two sticks of foil to form a cross) in the slow cooker, then pour in about 1 inch of boiling water. Set the baking dish on top. Cover and cook on low until a toothpick inserted into the center of the pudding comes out with some moist crumbs, 3 to 4 hours. Let cool to warm, then poke all over with a fork. Pour the reserved sauce over the top, and serve.

PREPARING PUDDINGS IN THE SLOW COOKER

One of the major advantages of slow cookers is that they rarely burn foods. However, burning can sometimes occur on food that sits against the insert's hot spot—the back interior surface of the crock, right in front of the heating element. Most susceptible to burning are dishes with a lot of sugar, eggs, or dry surfaces, or those that cook for 8 or more hours. When preparing puddings in the slow cooker, I follow one of two methods to prevent burning: line the slow cooker with several layers of heavy-duty aluminum foil or use a baking dish that fits in the insert.

To cook bread pudding directly in the slow cooker, measure the back inside surface of your insert, cut a rectangle of heavy duty aluminum foil that fits it, then use that as a template to create another five or so layers of foil. Overlap the layers and place over the area, pressing down to flatten. Add another two large pieces of foil perpendicular to one another, forming a cross inside the slow cooker and overlapping the sides. Press the foil flat against the inside walls of the crock, and bunch up the overlapping ends to serve as handles for removing the dish.

To prepare bread puddings and custard dishes in a baking dish that fits inside your slow cooker insert, use a water bath technique. Cover the baking dish tightly with foil, secure with thick rubber bands, and set the dish on a rack, trivet, or two crossed sticks made of foil placed inside the insert. Add boiling water to reach about halfway up the sides of the baking dish, then cover the slow cooker and cook.

Cinnamon-maple-apple dessert sauce

MAKES 5 CUPS

1 cup maple syrup

1 cup fresh apple cider

2 tablespoons tapioca starch

1 teaspoon ground cinnamon

½ teaspoon ground ginger

½ teaspoon coarse salt

8½ cups ½-inch-thick slices peeled and cored apples, such as McIntosh (about 8 medium)

This is the ultimate sweet applesauce or apple-cinnamon dessert sauce. It's terrific served over vanilla or pumpkin ice cream, gingerbread, or pancakes. You can always transfer it to a saucepan and simmer it over high heat to thicken it, but I love the consistency as is.

Mix together all of the ingredients except for the apples in the slow cooker. Add the apples, pushing them down to submerge in the liquid. Cover and cook on low until the apples are tender, 3½ to 4 hours. Mash with a potato masher.

Breakfast groats with pears, apples, and cinnamon

SERVES 10

Cooking spray

3 cups steel-cut groats

6 cups no-sugar-added apple juice

1 cup finely chopped sweetened dried pears

1 cup finely chopped unsweetened dried apples

1 teaspoon ground cinnamon

2 teaspoons coarse salt

¼ cup maple syrup

1 teaspoon vanilla bean paste or pure vanilla extract

Chopped toasted walnuts, for garnish (optional)

Chopped apples, for garnish (optional)

Chopped pears, for garnish (optional)

Sweetened dried coconut, for garnish (optional)

Chopped dates, for garnish (optional)

Raisins, for garnish (optional)

Whole milk or cream, for serving (optional)

Ideal for the day after Thanksgiving, this delicious breakfast entrée is easy, inexpensive, and high in yield. Set up a fixin's bar, and let guests add garnishes, such as chopped toasted nuts and milk or cream. If you make the groats in advance, reheat them with milk or apple juice.

Steel-cut groats can be found at health-food and some gourmet-food stores. Make sure to purchase steel-cut groats rather than whole groats (which take even longer to cook) or steel-cut oats. If you can only find the latter, know that they cook for less time.

Feel free to customize this recipe with other types of dried fruit and to swap in agave nectar or brown sugar for the maple syrup. If you make any changes, be sure to taste the groats and adjust the sweetness if necessary. Don't forget to add the water!

1. Spray the inside of the slow cooker with cooking spray, then add the groats, juice, 6 cups water, the dried pears, dried apples, cinnamon, and salt. Cover and cook on low until tender, about 8 hours.

2. Stir in the maple syrup and vanilla. Serve, adding garnishes, if desired.

Pears poached in mulled wine

SERVES 6

Zest of ½ large orange, in strips

1 teaspoon peeled chopped fresh ginger

1 cinnamon stick

8 whole cloves

1 star anise pod

5 black peppercorns

1 cup red wine, such as Merlot

1 cup ruby port

½ cup honey

¼ cup unsulfured molasses

Pinch of salt

6 firm pears, such as Bartlett or Bosc, peeled, halved, and cored

Serve these burnished purple pears with crème fraîche (with stirred-in orange zest and sugar or honey, if you like), ice cream, blue cheese, or gingerbread. It's best to prepare them ahead of time, so they soak up even more color and flavor from the cooking liquid.

Using thick, syrupy molasses and honey removes the need to reduce the liquid prior to poaching the pears. Feel free to vary the type of honey; for instance, try Italian chestnut honey for a darker, more complex dish.

1. Combine the zest, ginger, cinnamon, cloves, star anise, and peppercorns on a medium piece of cheesecloth and bundle into a bag, securing with kitchen twine. Set aside.

2. Stir together the rest of the ingredients except for the pears in the slow cooker, then add the pears, coating them with the sauce. Nestle in the spice bag. Cover and cook on low until the pears are very tender but still retain their shape, about 3 hours.

3. Carefully transfer the pears to a 9- x 13- x 2-inch baking dish (where they'll later marinate in the reduced cooking liquid). Pour the cooking liquid into a medium saucepan, discarding the cheesecloth bag. Boil over high heat until reduced to a scant 1¼ cups, 25 to 30 minutes (the sauce should slightly coat the back of a spoon). Pour the sauce over the pears in the baking dish and turn to coat. Let sit, covered, in the fridge for at least a couple of hours (marinating the pears will give them even more color and flavor). The pears can be served cold, at room temperature, or warm. When ready to serve them, transfer two pear halves to each plate and top with some poaching liquid.

Apple-date crisp with almonds

SERVES 8

¼ cup plus 3 tablespoons unsalted butter, at room temperature, divided

1 cup pure maple syrup

½ cup fresh-squeezed, strained orange juice (about 2 juicy oranges)

½ cup fresh apple cider

3 tablespoons tapioca starch

1 teaspoon almond extract

2 teaspoons ground cinnamon, divided

1½ teaspoons coarse salt, divided

6 cups ½-inch-thick slices peeled and cored baking apples, such as Macintosh (about 6)

1¼ cups quartered pitted fresh dates

1 cup all-purpose flour

1 cup unsalted almonds with skin, finely chopped

½ cup packed light brown sugar

Serve this traditional crisp with vanilla, ginger, or maple ice cream or with crème fraîche. Finishing the dessert in the oven thickens the juices and browns the crisp topping. Substitute pecans or walnuts for the almonds if you like. Be sure to taste the apples to gauge their sweetness, and adjust the seasoning accordingly.

1. Cut 2 tablespoons of the butter into about 8 cubes. In the slow cooker, mix together this cubed butter, the maple syrup, orange juice, cider, tapioca starch, almond extract, 1 teaspoon of the cinnamon, and ½ teaspoon of the salt. Mix in the apples and dates, flattening them down to one layer, so they're almost covered in liquid. Cover and cook on low until tender, about 4 hours.

2. Heat the oven to 350°F and grease a 9- x 13- x 2-inch baking dish with 1 table-spoon of the butter. Meanwhile, in a medium-size bowl, use your hands to crumble the remaining ¼ cup butter, remaining 1 teaspoon salt, remaining 1 teaspoon cinnamon, flour, almonds, and brown sugar. Carefully ladle the cooked apple mixture into the baking dish, and sprinkle evenly with the crumb topping. Bake until the topping is golden brown and the juices thicken and bubble, about 30 minutes. Serve while hot.

- **PREP TIME:** About 1 hour
- **SLOW COOKER TIME:** About 2 hours
- **PREP TIME FOR THE GLAZE:** About 10 minutes

Persimmon pudding with persimmon-lime glaze

SERVES 8

FOR THE PUDDING

½ stick unsalted butter, at room temperature, divided

7 to 10 extremely ripe Hachiya persimmons

1½ cups granulated sugar

1 tablespoon vanilla bean paste or pure vanilla extract

2 large eggs

¼ cup whole milk

2¼ cups all-purpose flour

2 teaspoons freshly grated lime zest (2 to 3 limes)

1½ teaspoons baking soda

1 teaspoon coarse salt

¾ teaspoon cinnamon

¼ teaspoon ground nutmeg

FOR THE GLAZE

½ cup plus 2 tablespoons confectioners' sugar

¼ cup fresh-squeezed, strained lime juice (about 2 juicy limes)

¼ cup mashed Hachiya persimmon flesh, 2 to 4 extremely ripe Hachiya persimmons

2 heaping teaspoons freshly grated lime zest

¼ teaspoon coarse salt

Vanilla ice cream, for serving

Persimmons add subtle fruitiness to this moist brown pudding, which looks and tastes like gingerbread. Gilded with an orange glaze specked with green lime zest, it's ideal served cold or warm—with ice cream, whipped cream, or crème fraîche. I love to microwave individual portions. You might want to reserve this dessert for a special occasion since it calls for a lot of fresh, pricey persimmons.

Be sure to use the ripest possible Hachiya persimmons. The fruit should be incredibly soft: black streaks on the outside indicate ripeness. If your persimmons aren't ripe, place them in a brown paper bag with an apple, then close it up tight and let sit overnight. Or, place in the freezer for a few hours; when they defrost, they'll be soft.

I prepared the pudding in my Pillivuyt 10½- x 7½- x 2-inch (1½-quart) oval baking dish; see the information on p. 211 for how to cook using this method.

1. Use 1 tablespoon of butter to grease the inside of a 1½-quart oval baking dish that will fit inside your slow cooker.

2. Over a graduated measuring cup, squeeze the persimmon flesh out of the skins, discarding the skins. Mash with a potato masher. Keep 2 cups, reserving any remaining flesh—if you have any—for the glaze.

3. In a stand mixer with the paddle attachment (or with a hand mixer), beat the remaining 3 tablespoons of butter and the sugar on medium-high speed until light and slightly fluffy, about 5 minutes. Add the vanilla and eggs, beating well to incorporate, about 1 minute. Add the persimmon flesh and milk and beat until combined, about 1 minute.

4. In a medium bowl, stir together the flour, zest, baking soda, salt, cinnamon, and nutmeg, and add to the mixing bowl. Beat on low speed just until combined, using a spatula to scrape down the sides of the bowl, about 1 minute.

5. Pour the batter into the prepared baking dish and cover tightly with aluminum foil. Place a rack or trivet in the bottom of the slow cooker and pour in about 1 inch of boiling water. Add the baking dish (the water should go about halfway up the sides). Cover the slow cooker and cook the pudding on high just until a fork poked into the center comes out clean, about 2 hours. Let sit for about 15 minutes before removing the baking dish (so you don't burn yourself).

6. About 10 minutes before the pudding will be finished cooking, combine all of the glaze ingredients in a medium-size mixing bowl; whisk vigorously until smooth. Pour over the top of the warm pudding, and serve portions with scoops of ice cream.

SPOTLIGHT ON

PERSIMMONS

Bright red-orange persimmons come in two varieties: Fuyu and Hachiya. Hachiya are shaped a bit like bell peppers; when not ripe, they taste very tannic and can dry out your mouth. When ripe—which you can tell because they'll be very soft and often streaked with black—they taste unbelievably sweet and delicious and will not give your mouth an unpleasant sensation. Fuyus are squat, small, a bit less sweet, and don't become soft when ripe. As a plus, though, they aren't astringent when unripe. I turn to Hachiyas most often. Both types of persimmons, grown in the United States and abroad, are available at most supermarkets.

Metric Equivalents

LIQUID/DRY MEASURES

U.S.	METRIC
¼ teaspoon	1.25 milliliters
½ teaspoon	2.5 milliliters
1 teaspoon	5 milliliters
1 tablespoon (3 teaspoons)	15 milliliters
1 fluid ounce (2 tablespoons)	30 milliliters
¼ cup	60 milliliters
⅓ cup	80 milliliters
½ cup	120 milliliters
1 cup	240 milliliters
1 pint (2 cups)	480 milliliters
1 quart (4 cups; 32 ounces)	960 milliliters
1 gallon (4 quarts)	3.84 liters
1 ounce (by weight)	28 grams
1 pound	454 grams
2.2 pounds	1 kilogram

OVEN TEMPERATURES

°F	Gas Mark	°C
250	½	120
275	1	140
300	2	150
325	3	165
350	4	180
375	5	190
400	6	200
425	7	220
450	8	230
475	9	240
500	10	260
550	Broil	290

Index